362.29
NNNN
FLY

Sept '12

Inhalants and Solvents
Sniffing Disaster

ILLICIT AND MISUSED DRUGS

Abusing Over-the-Counter Drugs:
Illicit Uses for Everyday Drugs

Addiction in America:
Society, Psychology, and Heredity

Addiction Treatment: Escaping the Trap

Alcohol Addiction: Not Worth the Buzz

Cocaine: The Rush to Destruction

Dual Diagnosis: Drug Addiction and Mental Illness

Ecstasy: Dangerous Euphoria

Hallucinogens: Unreal Visions

Heroin and Other Opioids:
Poppies' Perilous Children

Inhalants and Solvents: Sniffing Disaster

Marijuana: Mind-Altering Weed

Methamphetamine: Unsafe Speed

Natural and Everyday Drugs:
A False Sense of Security

Painkillers: Prescription Dependency

Recreational Ritalin: The Not-So-Smart Drug

Sedatives and Hypnotics: Deadly Downers

Steroids: Pumped Up and Dangerous

Tobacco: Through the Smoke Screen

Illicit and Misused Drugs

Inhalants and Solvents
Sniffing Disaster

by Noa Flynn

Mason Crest

Mason Crest
370 Reed Road
Broomall, Pennsylvania 19008
www.masoncrest.com

Copyright © 2013 by Mason Crest, an imprint of National Highlights, Inc. All rights reserved. No part of this publication may be reproduced or transmitted in any form or by any means, electronic or mechanical, including photocopying, recording, taping, or any information storage and retrieval system, without permission from the publisher.

Printed in the Hashemite Kingdom of Jordan.

First printing
9 8 7 6 5 4 3 2 1

Library of Congress Cataloging-in-Publication Data

Flynn, Noa.
Inhalants and solvents : sniffing disaster / Noa Flynn.
   p. cm. — (Illicit and misused drugs)
Includes bibliographical references and index.
ISBN 978-1-4222-2434-2 (hardcover)
ISBN 978-1-4222-2453-3 (paperback)
ISBN 978-1-4222-2424-3 (series hardcover)
ISBN 978-1-4222-9298-3 (ebook)
1. Inhalant abuse. I. Title.
RC568.S64F59 2012
362.29'93—dc23
                                    2011032587

Interior design by Benjamin Stewart.
Cover design by Torque Advertising + Design.
Produced by Harding House Publishing Services, Inc.
www.hardinghousepages.com

This book is meant to educate and should not be used as an alternative to appropriate medical care. Its creators have made every effort to ensure that the information presented is accurate—but it is not intended to substitute for the help and services of trained professionals.

CONTENTS

Introduction   6
1. Inhalants and Solvents: What They Are   9
2. Inhalants, Solvents, and the Body   23
3. Sniffing, Huffing, and Bagging: The Who and Why   49
4. Treatment for Inhalant and Solvent Addiction   77
5. It's More Than Just Say No   105

Glossary   117
Further Reading   121
For More Information   122
Bibliography   123
Index   126
Picture Credits   127
Author/Consultant Biographies   128

INTRODUCTION

Addicting drugs are among the greatest challenges to health, well-being, and the sense of independence and freedom for which we all strive—and yet these drugs are present in the everyday lives of most people. Almost every home has alcohol or tobacco waiting to be used, and has medicine cabinets stocked with possibly outdated but still potentially deadly drugs. Almost everyone has a friend or loved one with an addiction-related problem. Almost everyone seems to have a solution neatly summarized by word or phrase: medicalization, legalization, criminalization, war-on-drugs.

For better and for worse, drug information seems to be everywhere, but what information sources can you trust? How do you separate misinformation (whether deliberate or born of ignorance and prejudice) from the facts? Are prescription drugs safer than "street" drugs? Is occasional drug use really harmful? Is cigarette smoking more addictive than heroin? Is marijuana safer than alcohol? Are the harms caused by drug use limited to the users? Can some people become addicted following just a few exposures? Is treatment or counseling just for those with serious addiction problems?

These are just a few of the many questions addressed in this series. It is an empowering series because it provides the information and perspectives that can help people come to their own opinions and find answers to the challenges posed by drugs in their own lives. The series also provides further resources for information and assistance, recognizing that no single source has all the answers. It should be of interest and relevance to areas of study spanning biology, chemistry, history, health, social studies and more. Its efforts to provide a real-world context for the information that is clearly presented but not overly simplified should be appreciated by students, teachers, and parents.

The series is especially commendable in that it does not pretend to pose easy answers or imply that all decisions can be made on the basis of simple facts: some challenges have no immediate or simple solutions, and some solutions will need to rely as much upon basic values as basic facts. Despite this, the series should help to at least provide a foundation of knowledge. In the end, it may help as much by pointing out where the solutions are not simple, obvious, or known to work. In fact, at many points, the reader is challenged to think for him- or herself by being asked what his or her opinion is.

A core concept of the series is to recognize that we will never have all the facts, and many of the decisions will never be easy. Hopefully, however, armed with information, perspective, and resources, readers will be better prepared for taking on the challenges posed by addictive drugs in everyday life.

— Jack E. Henningfield, Ph.D.

1 Inhalants and Solvents: What They Are

I never thought it could happen to me. Becoming addicted to inhalants was not a plan that I had. I had a pretty good childhood, playing sports and hanging out with my brother and neighborhood friends. My mom and I were close, and we would spend quite a bit of time together.

My family lives in a fairly small, close-knit community where there were always fun activities planned for the kids. When I was 12 years old and entering seventh grade, . . . my life went down hill. I, Megan—you know, the girl next door—had many problems. Although a lot of teens probably feel as though they have problems, mine were rooted in something that wasn't my fault: sexual abuse. Dealing with something such as this, alone, is virtually an impossible task, and at the time, it felt impossible to overcome. Therefore, I needed

Inhalants are chemicals that are inhaled for non-medical purposes. They include many common household items.

10 Chapter 1—Inhalants and Solvents: What They Are

to cope. Life was becoming too much for me, and when I was offered help to begin a healing process, I refused it. I felt nothing at that time would help, until I encountered drugs.

Shortly after my 13th birthday, an older kid in the neighborhood who knew I was struggling offered me some weed. He thought it would help. So did I. It really seemed as though getting high was helping me forget my problems. Although, without even noticing, soon, I needed more drugs to get high. That's when I began huffing. . . . I inhaled almost anything I could get my hands on . . . so I could get high.

This is the beginning of Megan Hakeman's story of her addiction to inhalants, as she writes on the Partnership for a Drug-Free America website (www.drugfree.org/Teen/teen_3.html). Megan is just one of many teens—and those younger—who have abused products found in almost every household or office.

What Are Inhalants?

Put simply, inhalants are any chemicals that are intentionally taken into the body for nonmedical purposes by inhaling. Products such as vegetable cooking spray, model glue, nail polish remover, canned whipped cream, and hair spray all contain inhalants, breathable chemical vapors that can cause **psychoactive** effects. And these are only a few of the products that are popular among the population at large—as well as among those who choose to abuse drugs.

Inhalants can be divided into four categories. Volatile solvents are substances that **vaporize** at room temperature. In the context of inhalant abuse, volatile sub-

Products Abused as Inhalants

Volatile Solvents

adhesives
- model glue
- rubber cement
- household glue

aerosols
- spray paint
- hair spray
- air freshener
- deodorant
- fabric protector
- computer keyboard cleaner

solvents
- nail polish remover
- paint thinner
- typewriter correction fluid and thinner
- toxic markers
- pure toluene
- cigar lighter fluid
- gasoline
- carburetor cleaner
- octane booster

cleaning agents
- dry cleaning fluid
- spot remover
- degreaser

food products
- vegetable cooking spray
- dessert topping spray (whipped cream)
- whippets

gases
- nitrous oxide
- butane
- propane
- helium

anesthetics
- nitrous oxide
- ether
- chloroform

nitrites
- amyl
- poppers
- snappers
- butyl
- rush
- locker room
- bolt
- climax (video head cleaner)

(*Source*: National Inhalation Prevention Coalition. www.inhalants.org/product.htm.)

stances are further classified as industrial or household solvents and art or office supply solvents. Industrial or household solvents include such items as dry-cleaning fluid, degreaser, paint thinner, gasoline, and glue. Art or office supply solvents include correction fluid and felt-tip marker fluids.

Aerosol propellants are another category of inhalants. Among aerosol inhalants are spray paints, hair spray, deodorant spray, fabric protector spray, aerosol computer cleaning products, and vegetable cooking spray.

Gases used in household or commercial products or in the medical profession is another category of products abused for their mind-altering effects. Household or commercial products included under this category are **butane** lighters, propane tanks, whipping cream aerosols or **whippets**, and refrigerant gases among others. Medical gases with the potential for abuse as inhalants are involved in anesthesia. These include ether, chloroform, halothane, and nitrous oxide, often called laughing gas.

The last category of inhalants is nitrites. Substances in this category are not quite as well known and include amyl and butyl nitrites. Amyl nitrite, perhaps best known

Gases are one category of inhalants. They include household products such as propane tanks.

as "poppers" or "snappers" when used recreationally, is a clear, yellow liquid sold in cloth-covered sealed bulbs that make a snapping sound when broken. It may be used in the treatment of some heart conditions; a **vasodilator**, it also lowers blood pressure. Historically, it was used to treat **angina pectoris.** Amyl nitrite can also be used in treating **cyanide** poisoning. Amyl nitrite was available without a prescription until 1979.

Butyl nitrites are sold in small bottles with such names as "locker room" or "rush." It is similar to amyl nitrite, but its effects are not quite as strong. When a prescription became necessary for amyl nitrite, many recreational users switched to butyl nitrite.

How Inhalants Are Used

Their name says it all. These substances enter the body when they are inhaled. The fumes are taken into the body by:

- sniffing—inhaling the fumes from an open container
- huffing—inhaling the fumes from an inhalant-soaked cloth held to the user's face
- bagging—inhaling the fumes from a paper or plastic bag that is either held over the face or pulled over the user's head

In each case, the user's goal is to inhale the fumes as intensively as possible, and holding the inhalant as close to the face as possible is the prime way to do so. Of course, this can be a "tell" that someone is abusing inhalants, consider, for example, someone with paint all over his face.

Inhalants Timeline

800 BCE–392 CE	Oracle of Delphi inhales what are believed to have been ethylene vapors and enters a trance to answer questions or make prophesies
1275	Ether was discovered by Spanish chemist Raymundus Lullius and named "sweet vitriol"
1772	Nitrous oxide gas first discovered by English scientist Joseph Priestly
1831–1832	Chloroform was discovered independently by three scientists: Samuel Guthrie, Justus von Liebig, and Eugene Soubeiran. Originally it was used as a treatment for arthritis.
c.1840	Ether is used as a social lubricant during parties called "Ether Frolics"
Late 1940s	First known outbreak of gasoline sniffing in Warren, Pennsylvania
1950s	Reports of many cases of deliberate inhalation of gasoline fumes by young people in the United States, Australia, India, and Great Britain
1959	Earliest known references to glue sniffing in either medical or popular literature
1960s	An increasing number of newspaper articles report adolescents sniffing airplane glue
1960	The FDA [Food and Drug Administration] eliminates the prescription status of alkyl nitrites, making it available over the counter
1961–1965	Glue-sniffing epidemic in Denver. The epidemic may have been caused by hyperbolic media reports about the activity. Reports of glue sniffing soon spread to other U.S. cities
January 6, 1962	First known law against glue sniffing is passed in Anaheim, California
January 28, 1962	First peer-reviewed journal article on recreational glue sniffing appeared in the *Journal of the American Medical Association*
c.1967	Increasing reports of the recreational inhalation of aerosol products
1968	13 states and 29 counties and municipalities have passed anti glue-sniffing legislation

1969	The FDA reinstates the prescription status of amyl nitrite. Rumors suggest this was done in part because its maker was concerned about recreational use among homosexuals and how that might impact their image.
1977	Butyl nitrite sales exceed $50 million per year according to the *Wall Street Journal*
1981	FDA issues an official statement regarding nitrite odorants, stating that no regulations or restrictions are necessary because of the "absence of demonstrable hazard"

Each generation likes to believe that they have discovered something new—regardless of whether it is good or bad. Although some of the substances used for recreational purposes are fairly new, the use of inhalants is not.

Inhalants and the Oracle: Sniffing Out the Future?

The use of inhalants goes back to **antiquity**. Many researchers believe that the use of inhalants for nonmedical purposes can be traced to the Oracle of Delphi. U.S. geologists believe that the "trances" that brought forth the Oracle's predictions came from something a bit more earthly than spiritual.

As far back as 1400 BCE, the Oracle of Delphi was the most important shrine in Greece. Delphi was constructed around a sacred spring, and Greeks and Romans considered the site to be the center of the world. They came to Delphi from throughout the region, seeking answers to questions ranging from when to plant crops to when to start a war. According to the Greek writer Plutarch, who also served as the high priest during the first century CE,

The Oracle of Delphi was a shrine where ancient Greeks went to have questions answered by the Pythia. Modern geologists believe that the Pythia's trance was the result of inhalation of ethylene gas rising from a fault below the shrine.

18 Chapter 1—Inhalants and Solvents: What They Are

Dating Systems and Their Meaning

You might be accustomed to seeing dates expressed with the abbreviations BC or AD, as in the year 1000 BC or the year AD 1900. For centuries, this dating system has been the most common in the Western world. However, since BC and AD are based on Christianity (BC stands for Before Christ and AD stands for anno Domini, Latin for "in the year of our Lord"), many people now prefer to use abbreviations that people from all religions can be comfortable using. The abbreviations BCE (meaning Before Common Era) and CE (meaning Common Era) mark time in the same way (for example, 1000 BC is the same year as 1000 BCE, and AD 1900 is the same year as 1900 CE), but BCE and CE do not have the same religious overtones as BC and AD.

the source of these answers was a local woman called the Pythia, who went into a trance upon entering an underground chamber called the adyton.

Like answers given today by many claiming to have the ability to see into the future or to contact those who have "passed over," the Pythia's answers were often vague and subject to a multitude of interpretations. And if someone wasn't happy with the Pythia's insight into the future, more gold would get him another reading.

Delphi wasn't just a site to get predictions. Scholars often met there, and it developed a reputation as a place of intellectual sharing. Rivals sometimes met there to negotiate the settlement to a conflict, thereby avoiding war. Delphi also became home to many of Greece's art treasures. Hoping to curry favor with the Oracle, the Greek states sent their best—and most valuable—gifts to her.

However, the Oracle of Delphi's influence over the region lasted only until approximately 392 CE. When the Roman Empire became Christianized, Rome did not take kindly to the Oracle's prophesizing, and it ended.

Ethylene gas, in small doses, can cause euphoria and a sensation of floating. Unfortunately, some Pythia inhaled too much and died after entering the adyton at Delphi.

During Plutarch's service as the high priest in the first century, he left carefully detailed records about how the entire "prophesy process" worked. The Pythia would enter the adyton, and once inside, inhale what Plutarch referred to as sweet-smelling fumes from a *fissure* or spring. Sometimes after inhaling the fumes, the Pythia would go into a simple trance state, but at other times, she would experience delirium. Some Pythia were not so lucky and died after inhaling. Plutarch gave no real indication as to where the fumes came from, but did speculate that they *emanated* from rocks below the shrine.

In 2001, U.S. geologists reported findings from their discovery of a fault line running below the shrine. The geologists hypothesize that earthquake activity heated the limestone deposits, causing the release of hydrocarbon gases. A spring northwest of the shrine contains traces of ethylene, a sweet-smelling gas that, in small doses, can cause *euphoria* and the sensation of floating. Many historians and archaeologists now believe the Pythia received her insight with some help from the ethylene gas.

Though individuals who abuse inhalants today might not be looking for clues to the future, their bodies feel the same effects of the "all-seeing" Pythia.

CAUT
FLAMMABLE/

ATTEN
INFLAMMABLE

ACH OF CHILDREN/GARDE

2 Inhalants, Solvents, and the Body

DANGER
Extremely Flammable
Harmful or Fatal If Swallowed
Vapors May Cause Fire

Those words, or similar ones, appear on the labels of many inhalant products. Many labels also warn that the product should be used only in a well-ventilated area. It's surprising people aren't scared away from using the products. It's even more amazing that these warnings don't deter some individuals from using these inhalants for reasons other than those for which they are intended. In order to appreciate how dangerous these products are, it's necessary to know how they affect the body when used incorrectly.

The Basics

In the world of misused products, inhalants are very effective at creating a high. They work on the body very quickly. Effects can be felt as quickly as a few seconds; at the most, it might take a few minutes to achieve a high. How quickly someone feels the effects depends on the type of inhalant and how its fumes are breathed in. Sniffing provides the lowest concentration, and bagging gives the user the highest concentration of fumes.

Inhalants quickly pass through lung tissue and enter the bloodstream. Once in the bloodstream, the chemicals easily cross the blood–brain barrier, a mechanism intended to keep harmful substances from passing from the blood to the brain. This transfer can occur so quickly that it mimics the intense effects produced from **intravenous** injection of psychoactive drugs. Like alcohol, most inhalants are **sedatives**, and someone under their effects can resemble a person who has had too much alcohol to drink: decreased **inhibitions** and depression when enough is consumed.

Many inhalants contain more than one chemical, and how that inhalant affects the body depends in part on what chemicals it contains. Three common chemicals are toluene, fluorocarbons, and nitrous oxide.

Toluene

Toluene is a petroleum-based product and is found in wood smoke emissions. The colorless, flammable product is used in at least thirteen industries, including consumer products, furnishings, building materials, and pesticides. It is often found in canned **octane** boosters (also called "race formula"), as well as in food flavorings, sweeteners, and paint. And, it's the last T in trinitrotoluene—TNT the explosive, not the television network.

Inhalants are very effective at creating a high because they work on the body so quickly. Effects may be felt after only a few seconds.

Not a Laughing Matter

"Laughing gas." It sounds innocent enough—perhaps even a good thing. How many times have you seen someone in a film or on television sitting in a dentist's chair laughing at each and every little thing, truly funny or not? It might seem obvious, but that is not a real-life situation. When dentists and physicians use nitrous oxide, it is mixed with oxygen. When inhaled, pure nitrous oxide binds to the oxygen carried in your bloodstream. This means that the oxygen your body needs to function can't get into the tissues. Nitrous oxide intended to be misused for its mind-altering properties generally isn't cut with oxygen. Instead, you'll often find it contains sulfuric acid, ammonia, or nitric oxide. All are poisonous and can make you very ill—or dead.

Fluorocarbon

A fluorocarbon is a **halocarbon** in which fluorine has replaced one or more of the hydrogen atoms. Fluorocarbons are used in many products, including anesthetics, refrigerants, propellants, solvents, lubricants, and water and stain repellants. Fluorocarbons are long-lasting, remaining part of the environment long past their original use.

Nitrous Oxide

Perhaps more recognizable when called "laughing gas," nitrous oxide is also known as dinitrogen oxide and dinitrogen monoxide. It is a colorless, nonflammable chemical compound, with a slightly sweet odor. It is an approved food additive, most commonly used as a propellant in such canned products as whipped cream. It is also approved for use as an **inert gas** to replace oxygen in bags of snack products such as potato chips. Beyond the food industry, nitrous oxide is sometimes used as an **oxidizer**

Nitrous oxide, or laughing gas, is familiar as the anesthetic sometimes used by dentists. This colorless gas is also used to replace oxygen in bags of snack foods.

Inhalants and Solvents—Sniffing Disaster

Toluene is a chemical commonly found in inhalants. This petroleum-based product is found in wood smoke as well as many consumer products and dynamite.

in internal combustion engines (where it is known as nitrous or NOS) or in rocket engines. It is used in dentistry and in some minor surgeries as an anesthetic and for its pain-relieving qualities. Nitrous oxide occurs naturally in the atmosphere. It is one of the greenhouse gases, which contributes to the **greenhouse effect**, which has become a major environmental problem.

These and other chemicals interact in the inhalants to affect the body in many ways.

Inhalants in the Body

The National Inhalant Prevention Coalition lists on its website (www.inhalants.org/guidelines.htm) four stages in the development of symptoms related to solvent abuse:

A. Stage One—Excitatory Stage:
Symptoms include: euphoria, excitation, exhilaration, dizziness, **hallucinations**, sneezing, coughing, excess salivation, **photosensitivity**, nausea, vomiting, flushed appearance, and bizarre behavior.

B. Stage Two—Early Central Nervous System Depression:
Symptoms include: confusion, disorientation, dullness, loss of self-control, ringing or buzzing in the head, blurred or double vision, cramps, headache, insensitivity to pain, and **pallor** or paleness.

C. Stage Three—Medium Central Nervous System Depression:
Symptoms include: drowsiness, muscular uncoordination, slurred speech, depressed reflexes, and **nystagmus**.

There are four stages in the symptoms of inhalant abuse. Excitation and euphoria may be seen in Stage One.

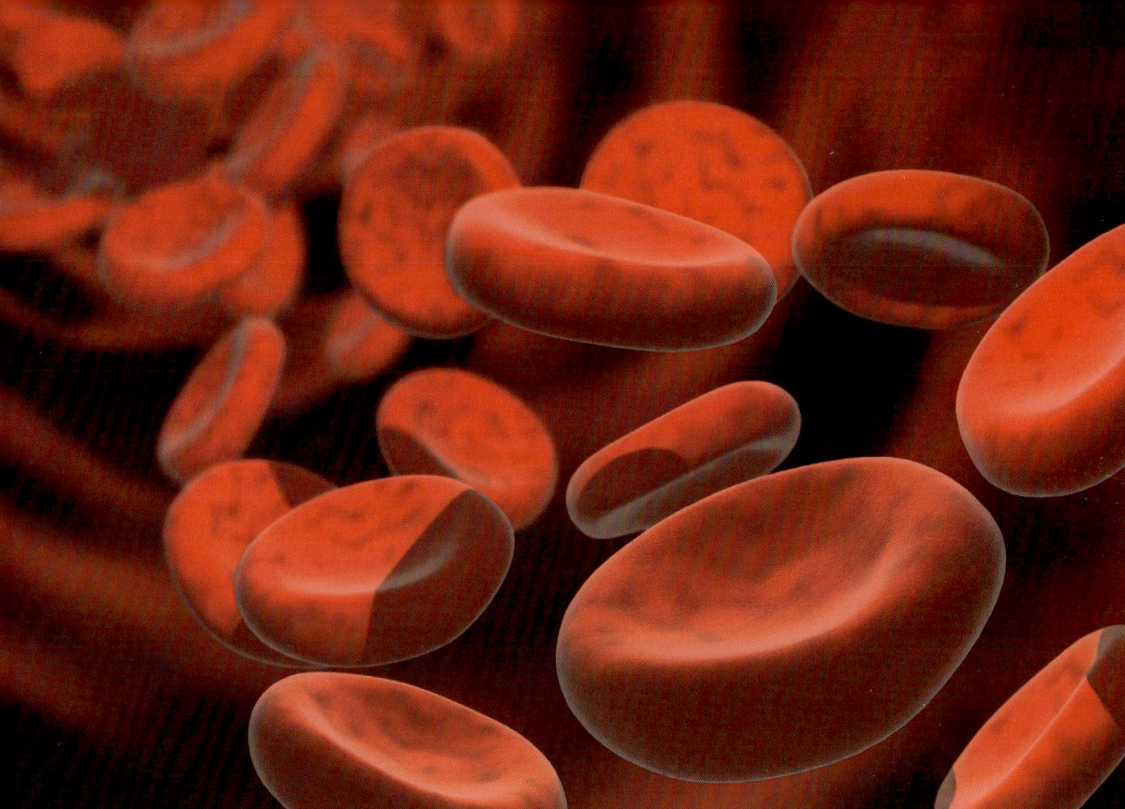

Inhalants affect the body very quickly. The reason for this is their ability to enter the bloodstream and cross the blood-brain barrier.

D. Stage Four—Late Central Nervous System Depression: Symptoms include: unconsciousness that may be accompanied by strange dreams, epileptiform seizures and **electroencephalogram (EEG)** changes.

As mentioned earlier in this chapter, the effects of inhalants are felt very quickly because of their ability to enter the bloodstream and cross the blood–brain barrier. The most commonly abused inhalants act on the brain and spinal cord, the body's central nervous system (CNS), and the body's functions are slowed, the depression indicated in the symptom stages listed above. Which part of the CNS is affected by the inhalant depends on its ingredients.

One of the biggest areas of concern to scientists studying the effects of inhalant abuse on the brain is how they affect the body's nerve cells. Some of the ingredients contained in inhalants are eliminated from the body quickly. Those that get absorbed in the fatty tissues in the CNS can stay there, affecting the individual, for a long time.

The body is a complex machine, and its communication system equally so. Almost every inch of the human body is touched by nerve fibers, made up of nerve cells, or neurons. These are major components in the communication system that controls almost every facet of the body's thinking and doing process. Each nerve cell consists of a cell body with an axon, a whip-like tail, at one end and root-looking projections called dendrites at the other end. Surrounding the axons is a thick, fatty tissue called the myelin sheath, which is also a popular stopping-off place for chemicals such as toluene. It acts to protect the nerve cells. For messages to get where they need to go, they must travel along the axon. When a disease process such as multiple sclerosis occurs or when someone abuses inhalants, the myelin sheath can become eroded or destroyed, and the nerves are less able to send messages. Some may not get where they are needed, and others can become garbled, sending out the wrong signals. When cell death occurs, the resulting effects depend on where in the brain that death occurs. If it happens in the cerebral cortex—the outer layer of the front part of the brain that is responsible for perception of sensations, learning, reasoning, and memory—the abuser may experience permanent personality changes, memory loss, hallucinations, and learning disabilities. Once cell death occurs in the cerebellum—the part of the brain responsible for the control of balance and muscle coordination—slurred

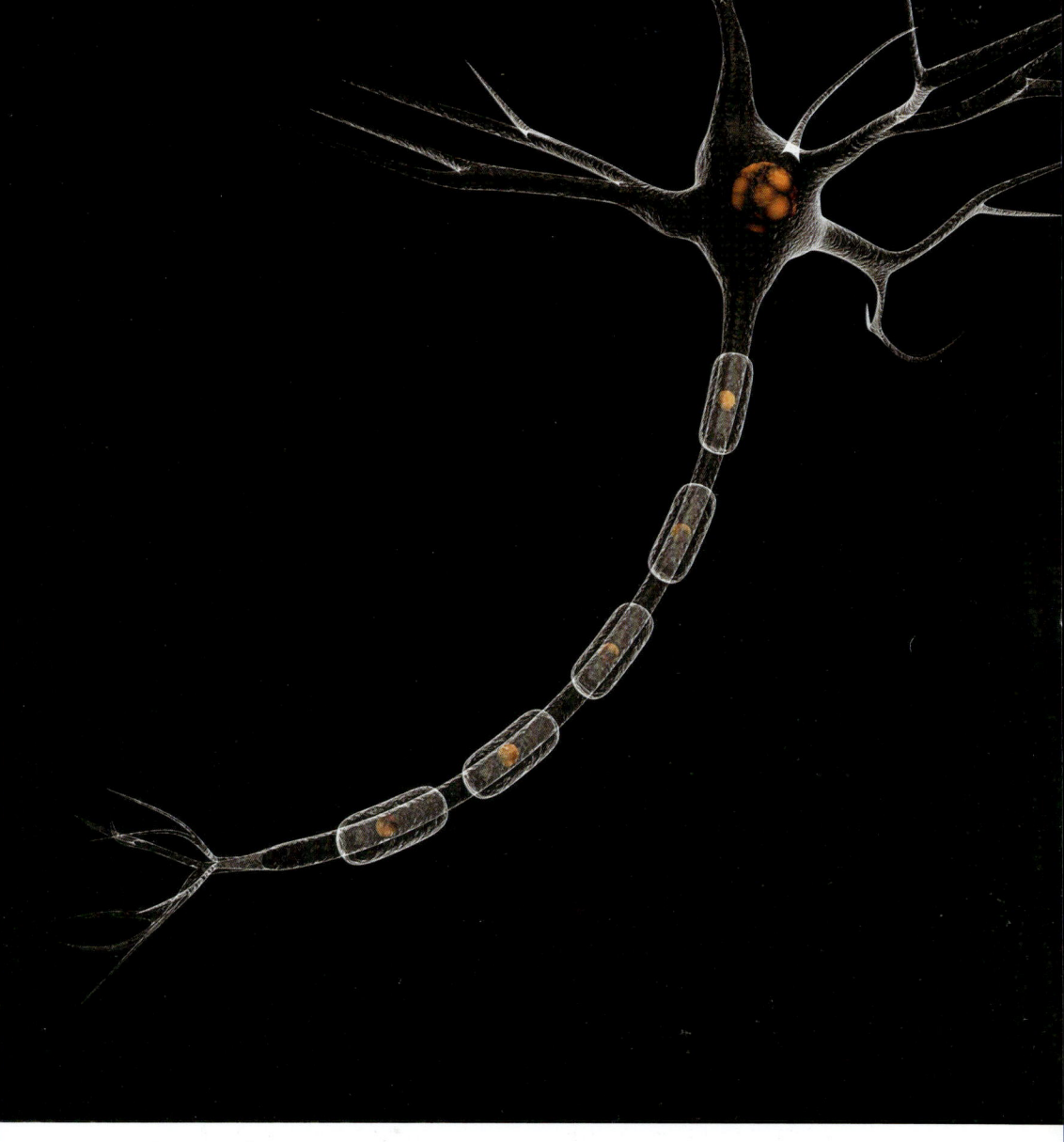

A nerve cell is a major component of the body's communication system. If damaged by disease, or inhalant abuse, neurons may not be able to send clear messages.

speech and loss of coordination can result. Toluene may also adversely affect the ophthalmic nerve, which can result in visual disorders.

Cocaine or Inhalants: Surprising Findings

For some time, researchers associated long-term or chronic inhalant abuse with brain damage and intellectual impairment that ranged from a slight impairment to full-blown *dementia*. A 2002 study funded by the National Insti-

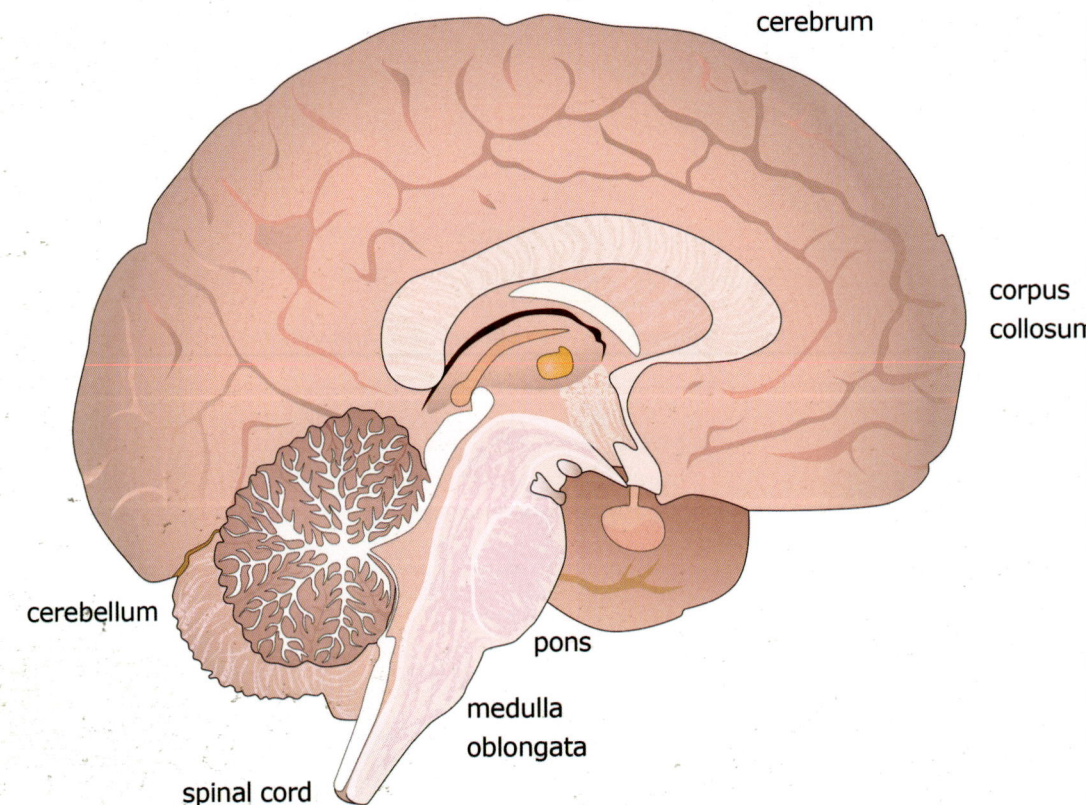

Chemicals like toluene degrade the protective myelin sheath of nerve cells, which results in cell death. The effects of this depend on where in the brain cell death occurs.

tute on Drug Abuse (NIDA) determined the extent of brain damage caused by the abuse of inhalants. The study compared the amount of brain damage and intellectual functioning impairment between chronic users of volatile solvents and cocaine. As might be expected, it was discovered that both groups suffered from brain damage and *compromised* intellectual functioning. What came as a surprise to some was that inhalant abusers had more abnormalities and more serious brain damage, as shown in magnetic resonance imaging (MRI) scans. Although both the cocaine users and inhalant abusers scored below the general public, inhalant abusers had greater difficulty successfully completing tasks that tested memory and the ability to focus, plan, and solve problems.

The inhalant abusers who participated in the study used mostly spray paint. On average, they had been regularly abusing inhalants for ten years. The study participants classified their use level as ranging from "sporadic and intense" to "continuously"; more than 50 percent admitted to being high on inhalants for most of every day.

Inhalants' Effects on Other Parts of the Body

Inhalants' ill effects are not limited to the brain. Nitrites and methylene chloride bind to oxygen molecules in the body and prevent the oxygen in the bloodstream from getting to the body's tissues where it is needed. Every organ in the body requires oxygen to function properly; so, when they are oxygen deprived, the organs cannot work to their optimal capacity. Lung damage can be caused by aerosols such as spray paint. Inhalation of products containing *halogenated* compounds (spray paint and typewriter correction fluid, for example) can lead to liver

Adverse Effects of Inhalants

Cardiovascular Effects
dysrhythmias
hypoxia-induced heart block
myocardial fibrosis
sudden sniffing death syndrome

Dermatological Effects
burns
contact dermatitis
perioral eczema

Gastrointestinal Effects
hepatotoxicity
nausea or vomiting

Hematologic Effects
aplastic anemia
bone marrow suppression
leukemia

Neurologic Effects
ataxia
cerebellar degeneration
change in speech
nystagmus
peripheral neuropathy
sensorimotor polyneuropathy
tremor
white matter degeneration

Neuropsychiatric Effects
apathy
dementia
depression
insomnia
memory loss
poor attention
psychosis

Pulmonary Effects
cough or wheezing
dyspnea
emphysema
goodpasture's syndrome
pneumonitis

Renal Effects
acid-based disturbance
acute renal failure
Fanconi's syndrome
renal tubular acidosis

(*Source:* Anderson and Loomis, 2003.)

---

damage. Kidney damage is a frequent result of using toluene-containing inhalants. Individuals who sniff gasoline and other products containing benzene are more prone to develop some forms of blood disorders, including leukemia and **aplastic anemia**. The muscles are affected by long-term inhalant abuse. One muscle in particular—the heart—plays a significant role in one of the most serious side effects of inhalant abuse.

Side Effects of Inhalant Abuse

Consider Kyle Williams, a 14-year-old who kissed his mom goodnight and headed to his room one evening in March 2005. The next morning his mother went in to wake Kyle up. Instead, she found him dead in bed, with a straw from a can of computer cleaner he had inhaled still in his mouth. One of Kyle's friends had shown him how to get

A study conducted by NIDA determined that inhalant abuse actually causes more extensive brain damage than cocaine abuse.

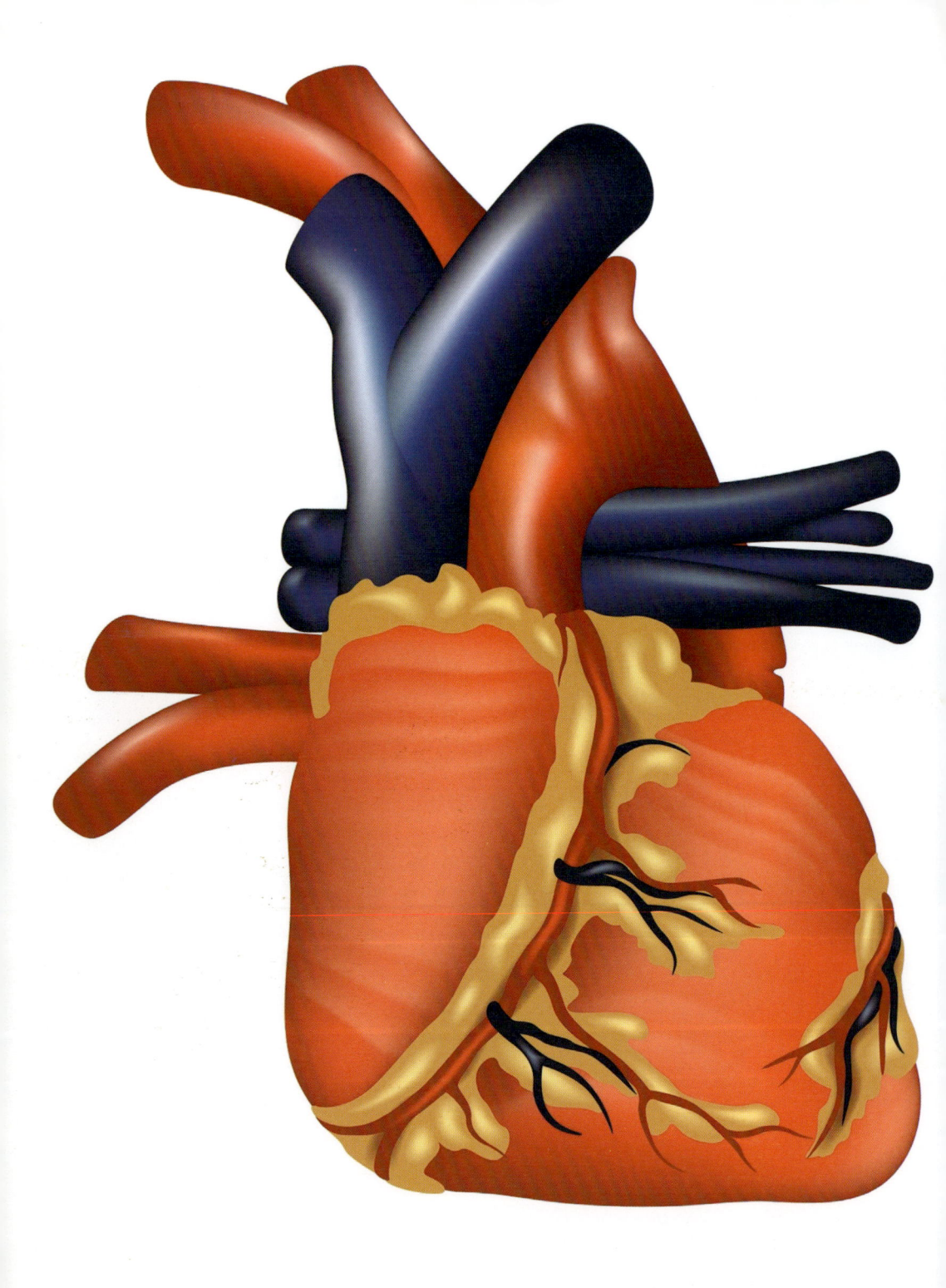

One of the most serious potential side effects is sudden sniffing death. This occurs when the heart's rhythm becomes irregular and can cause heart failure and death.

high this way about a month before. Some might think such cans contain nothing but compressed air. They couldn't be more mistaken.

As the above story from the November 1, 2005, issue of *Scholastic Choices* shows, some side effects of inhalant abuse can be deadly. In Kyle's case, it is likely that he died as a result of "sudden sniffing death," one short-term side effect that many who participate in sniffing, huffing, or bagging activities have no idea can happen. And, it can happen the very first time someone abuses inhalants.

Sudden sniffing death usually occurs after a session of prolonged sniffing. In most cases, the solvents are inhaled in highly concentrated forms. After a while, the inhalants can cause the heart's rhythm to become irregular and to beat too quickly, causing the individual to go into heart failure and possibly die.

In 2009, inhalant abuse brought more than 6,000 individuals into hospital emergency departments across the United States. According to the Drug Abuse Warning Network (DAWN), there were 6,137 inhalant-related emergency department notations. To be considered a DAWN case, the drug has to be implicated in the reason for the trip to the emergency department; it does not have to be the direct cause of the visit.

Other short-term physical side effects of inhalant abuse include:

- slurred speech
- relaxation
- euphoria
- hallucinations
- drowsiness

Inhalant abuse causes many short-term physical side effects. These can range from relaxation and drowsiness to euphoria, from hallucinations to dizziness and nausea.

- dizziness
- nausea
- vomiting
- death
- blackouts caused by rapidly changing blood pressure

Besides that caused from sudden sniffing death, individuals can die from suffocating on plastic bags used for huffing or bagging, or from inhaling their own vomit.

Some of the side effects caused by long-term or chronic abuse of inhalants have been discussed previously in this chapter. Others include weight loss, fatigue, *electrolyte* imbalance, and muscle fatigue. Although all side effects are serious, it is possible to reverse some conditions. These include liver and kidney damage and blood oxygen depletion. However, not all long-term side effects can be reversed simply by stopping the abuse of inhalants. These side effects include hearing loss, peripheral **neuropathies** or spasms, CNS or brain damage, and bone marrow damage.

Long-term or chronic use of inhalants can cause tolerance to build up in the person who is abusing them. When this occurs, the user finds that it takes increasing amounts of inhalants to achieve the same result. In some cases, individuals abusing inhalants must change the way the substance enters their body. For example, perhaps in the beginning the abuser reached an "acceptable" high by sniffing. But, after a while, he doesn't get the same sensation he did when he began sniffing. So, he can either change the substance, or he can change to bagging, a method in which the inhalant is taken into the body in a more concentrated—stronger—form.

Nitrites have special risks involved in their use. Primary users of nitrites are older teenagers and adults looking to increase their sexual pleasures. Some research has shown that certain side characteristics of using nitrites, such as a lessening of inhibitions, can lead to unsafe sexual practices and leave individuals susceptible to HIV/AIDS and other sexually transmitted diseases.

A possible link between nitrite-containing inhalants and the development and growth of tumors and infectious diseases has been found in animal research studies. It has been proven that the inhalation of nitrites destroys many of the cells making up the immune system, making the body less able to fight off disease. Animal research also showed that it takes only limited exposure to butyl nitrite to significantly increase the number of tumors, as well as to speed up the rate of tumor growth.

Not all side effects of inhalant abuse are physical. Psychological and behavioral side effects of inhalant abuse include:
- impaired judgment
- mental confusion
- fright
- hyperactivity
- anxiety
- acute *psychosis*
- increased violent or aggressive behavior

Potentially harmful chemicals are found in many common household products. Canned whipped cream, for example, contains nitrous oxide.

Things You Need to Know About Inhalants

1. Household products can be dangerous. Inhalants are breathable chemical vapors that produce mind-altering effects. Some of these come from everyday household products like spray paint, glues, and cleaning fluids. But these toxic chemicals were never meant to be inside a human body.
2. Using inhalants just one time can kill you. Sniffing highly concentrated amounts of the chemicals in solvents or aerosol sprays can cause heart attacks and even death within minutes.
3. No matter how inhalants are taken, they still spell danger. There is no safe way to breathe toxic fumes.
4. Your brain may never be the same again. The poison in inhalants can kill so many brain cells that brain tissue actually shrinks. People who abuse inhalants may have difficulty with memory, learning, and thinking.
5. When you hurt your brain, you hurt your body. Inhalants dissolve the protective coating called myelin on the neurons, or cells in the brain. When myelin is damaged, messages move too slowly—resulting in muscle spasms, tremors, and even difficulty walking and talking.
6. By using inhalants, you risk depression. The sniffer can fall into a gloomy mood where nothing about life seems good or hopeful.
7. You can lose your hearing for good. Use of toluene (a chemical found in spray paint and glue) and trichloroethylene (a chemical found in cleaning fluids and correction fluids) can cause hearing loss.
8. The destruction could go as deep as inside your bones; use of benzene (or gasoline) can damage bone marrow.
9. Damage can go beyond your brain and bones. Chronic exposure to inhalants can lead to significant damage to the heart, lungs, liver, and kidneys.

(*Source:* From Junior Scholastic, January 5, 2004.)

The best way—and the only 100 percent effective way—of preventing short- and long-term side effects is never to abuse inhalants. Or, if a friend or relative is abusing inhalants, help them stop. According to the Consumer Product Safety Commission and the National

Inhalant Prevention Coalition, signs that someone might be abusing inhalants include:

- burning sensation on the tongue
- dazed, dizzy, or drunken-seeming appearance
- nausea and/or loss of appetite
- neurologic problems including peripheral neuropathy, loss of vision, severe cognitive impairment, and seizures
- red or runny eyes and/or nose
- signs of paint, correction fluid, or other chemical products in unusual places, such as the face or fingers
- slurred or disoriented speech
- unusual behaviors such as anxiety, irritability, anger, excitability, or restlessness with no **discernable** cause
- unusual odor on the breath or chemical odor on clothing

They may also begin using street names for some of the inhalants:

Air blast	heart-on
Ames	Hiagra in a bottle
amys	highball
aroma of men	hippie crack
bolt	huff
boppers	laughing gas
bullet	locker room
bullet bolt	Medusa
buzz bomb	moon gas
discorama	Oz
hardware	pearls

poor man's pot
poppers
quicksilver
rush snappers
Satan's secret
shoot the breeze
snappers
snotballs

spray
Texas shoe shine
thrust
toilet water
toncho
whippets
whiteout

Inhalants found in out-of-the ordinary places or amounts can also be a sign of inhalant abuse.

Despite the dangers associated with inhalant abuse, it continues to be a problem. And, the abusing population has some unique characteristics.

Harmful Effects of Inhalants

Inhalant	Harmful Effects
Toluene	hearing loss
	damage to central nervous system
	liver and kidney damage
Trichloroethylene	hearing loss
	liver and kidney damage
	vision damage
Hexane	limb spasms
	blackouts
Nitrous Oxide	limb spasms
	blackouts
Benzene	bone marrow damage
	immune system damage

(*Source: Scholastic Choices*, November 1, 2005.)

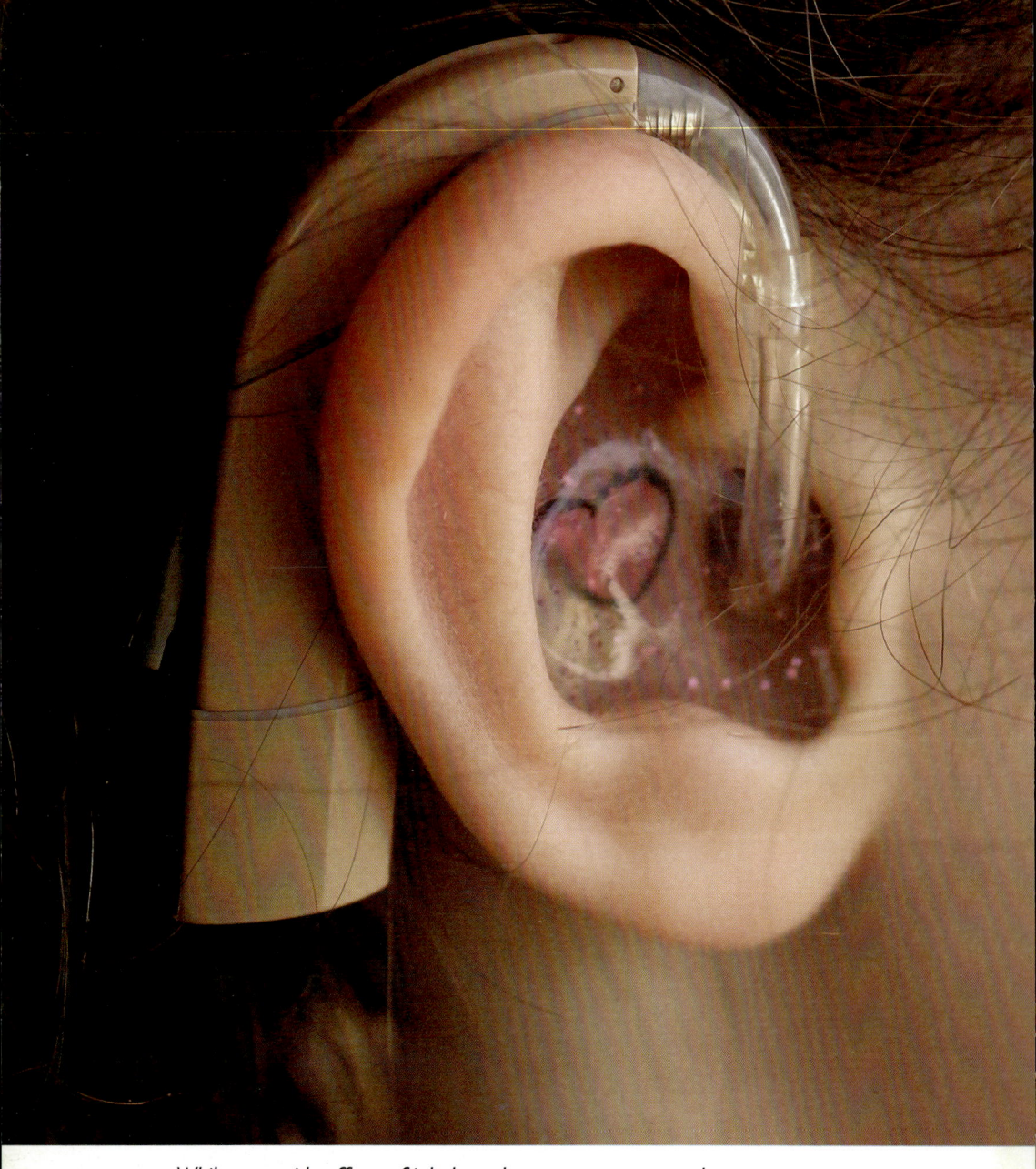

While some side effects of inhalant abuse are temporary, others are permanent. Hearing loss, for example, is irreversible.

46 Chapter 2—Inhalants, Solvents, and the Body

Chemicals Found in Inhalants

Products	Harmful Chemicals
Aerosols	
spray paint	butane, propane, fluorocarbons, hydrocarbons, toluene
hair spray	butane, propane, fluorocarbons
deodorants	butane, propane, fluorocarbons
analgesic spray	fluorocarbons
asthma spray	fluorocarbons
Anesthetics	
gaseous	nitrous oxide, chloroform
liquid	halothane, enflurane
local	ethyl chloride
Cleaning Agents	
dry cleaning	tetrachloroethylene, trichloroethane
spot removers	tetrachloroethylene, trichloroethane
degreasers	tetrachloroethylene, trichloroethane, trichloroethylene
Solvents	
fingernail polish remover	acetone
paint remover	acetone, toluene, methylene chloride, methanol, XYLOL, naptha, turpentine, hexane
paint thinners	toluene, methylene chloride, methanol, naptha
correction fluid	toluene, methylene chloride, methanol
fuel	gasoline, butane, propane
lighter	butane, isopropane
fire extinguisher	bromochlorodifluoromethane
Food Products	
whipped cream	nitrous oxide
whippets	nitrous oxide
Nitrite Room Odorizers	
Locker room, Rush, Poppers, Bolt,	(iso)amyl nitrite, (iso)butyl nitrite, (iso)propyl nitrite,
Climax	butyl nitrite

(Source: www.neonjoint.com.)

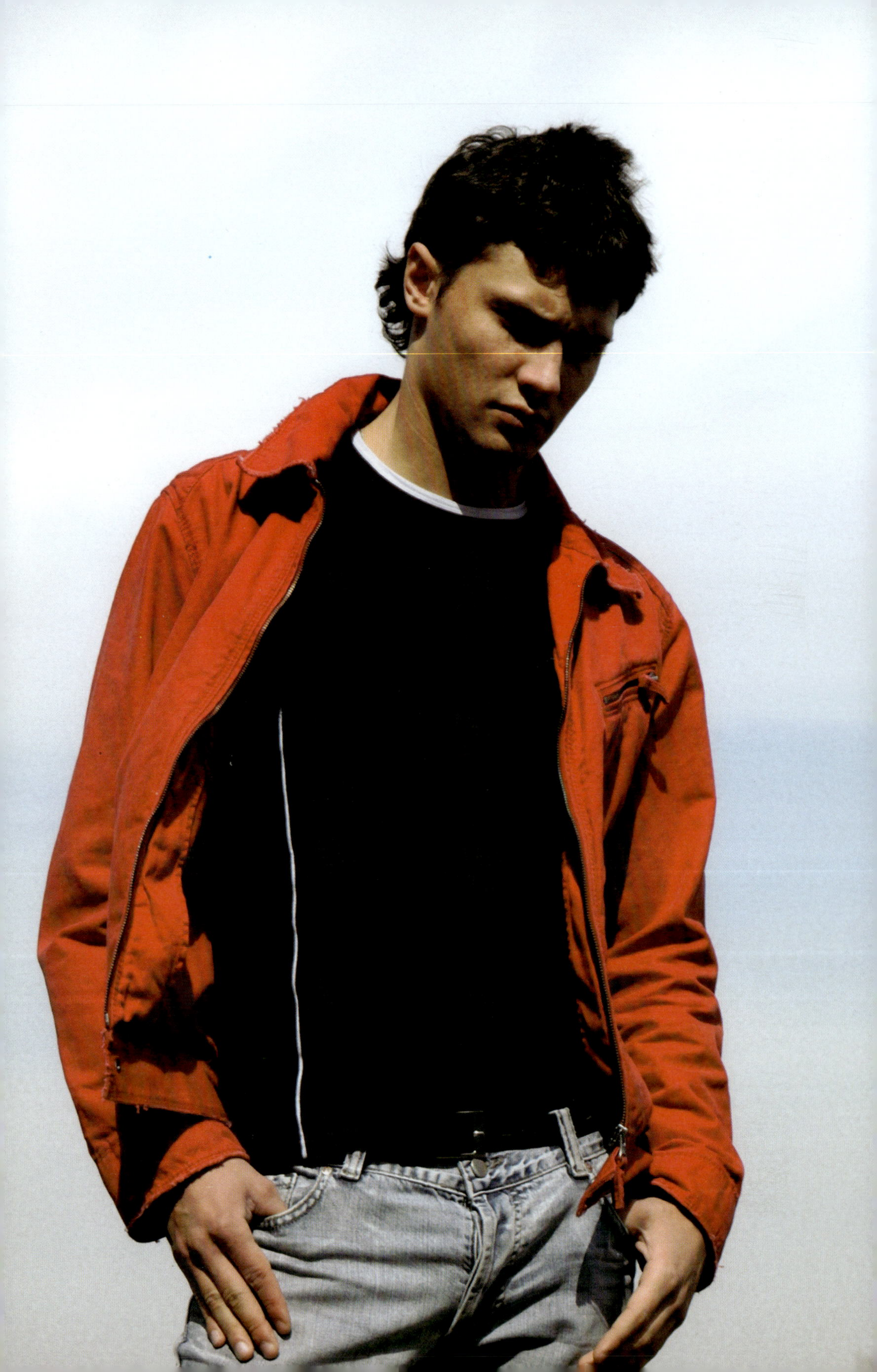

3 Sniffing, Huffing, and Bagging: The Who and Why

The next time you are in New York City my wife and I would like to invite you to stop in and see our son. He hangs out in a gallery just off One Times Square between West 46th and 47th Streets and would welcome a visit. His name is David and he's a handsome boy, not very tall at 5´8´´, but with incredible hazel eyes and a smile that will melt your heart. You'll enjoy meeting him and learning about his dreams and the things that are important to a boy his age. He wants to be an orthopedic surgeon like his grandfather. He loves baseball, has played catcher ever since he was in Pee Wee Little League and even started a few times on his high school team. And he's a big fan of Rap music too, Snoop Dog, Master P, Tupac, all fill his world with the rebelliousness and passion he shares with all sixteen year olds.

Sixteen you say. . . . Hmmmm . . . kind of young to be hanging out in a place like the Big Apple especially in Times Square in the heart of Manhattan. And of course you are absolutely right. You see his mother and I never wanted him to go there . . . not like this. We worked very hard to try and prevent him from making the decision that led him there. We worked with his friends from childhood, his girlfriend, and even sought professional help, but in the end it was his decision, one that he made alone, knowing full well what the consequences could be. A decision that was made with the surety of life as seen through the eyes of a 16 year-old, where bad things only happen to other people.

He drowned that warm sunny day in June 2001 getting high after inhaling the propellant from a can of computer duster. The poison in the propellant froze his heart and lungs and though they quickly pulled him from the pool, it was too late.

And now there his pictures are today, in that store front off of Times Square, part of the Drug Enforcement Agency's Lost Talent section of the "Target America: Drug Traffickers, Terrorists and You" traveling exhibit. Originally the "Lost Talent" section was to feature pictures only of famous people from film, art and music who have been lost to drug abuse.

Fortunately somewhere along the way a great idea got better when the decision was made to

The DEA created a traveling exhibit to showcase the dangers of drug abuse. Part of this exhibit includes images and stories of people whose lives were lost to drug abuse.

Inhalants and Solvents—Sniffing Disaster

include unknown people like Dave whose lost talent and potential has been devastating, not only to his family and friends, but to our society at large.

Two weeks before Dave died my wife asked him, in the midst of his struggle with addiction, what he wanted to do with his life? And with all the passion and sincerity that only those hazel eyes and that warm smile could radiate he said to her, "I want to make a difference in this world with my life."

And so you have, my son . . . and so you have.

It's probably safe to assume that most abusers of inhalants don't plan to end up like Dave, an image traveling in an exhibition about the dangers of doing drugs. Yet, the danger of drugs has not proven to be a deterrent to many looking for a way to get high. And, their search for an escape begins at a very young age.

Age of First Abuse

In 2009, the Monitoring the Future (MTF) survey found that, overall, illicit drug use was down among teenagers in the United States. This trend holds true for the use of inhalants, which has seen a decline since the 2005 survey. In 2005, the survey found that 17.1 percent of eighth-graders, 13.1 percent of tenth-graders, and 11.4 percent of twelfth-graders had used inhalants at least once during their lives. According to the 2011 MTF survey, use among all age groups had decreased, though eighth-graders still show the highest use. The use of inhalants by eighth-graders reflects one of the most alarming features of inhalant abuse: inhalants are often the first

Percentage of Students Reporting Inhalant Use, 2005

	8th Grade	10th Grade	12th Grade
Past month	4.2	2.2	2.0
Past year	9.5	6.0	5.0
Lifetime	17.1	13.1	11.4

(*Source:* Office of National Drug Control Policy. www.whitehousedrugpolicy.gov/drugfact/inhalants/index.html.)

drugs abused by young people. According to Dr. Edward C. Jauch on the website http://emedicine.medscape.com/article/1174630-overview, the average age of initial use of inhalants is ten, about eighteen months before the average person first tries cigarettes and four years before the average initial use of narcotics. The inhalant experimentation period generally occurs in late childhood and doesn't last long. Those who go on to use inhalants chronically usually do so during late adolescence and end by age nineteen or twenty. There are, however, some cases of inhalant abuse by individuals in their fifties and sixties.

The National Survey on Drug Use and Health (NSDUH) and MTF also asked adolescents in eighth and twelfth grades how risky they perceived abusing inhalants to be. Although most agreed occasional use was risky, fewer adolescents were apparently aware that even one-time use can cause serious problems, even death. Of those surveyed, 32 percent of eighth-graders and 41 percent of tenth-graders believed that there was a "great risk" of trying inhalants once or twice. Over 80 percent of all students say that they disapprove of ever trying an inhalant.

Grade	2001 (in percentage)	2003 (in percentage)	2005 (in percentage)
9	17.4	13.6	14.1
10	14.0	11.1	13.2
11	13.8	11.0	11.4
12	12.5	11.8	10.1
Total	14.7	12.1	12.4

Monitoring the Future

Since 1975, the Monitoring the Future (MTF) survey has measured drug, alcohol, and cigarette use and related attitudes among adolescent students nationwide. Survey participants report their drug use behaviors across three time periods: lifetime, past year, and past month. In 2011, the survey found that 10.6 percent of all eighth, tenth, and twelfth graders had tried inhalants in their lifetime. 5.0 percent had tried them in the last year. The survey is funded by the National Institute on Drug Abuse, a component of the National Institutes of Health, and conducted by the University of Michigan.

The age when inhalant abuse begins was also a factor on who became dependent on the substances. According to the NSDUH study, those who first used inhalants between the ages of thirteen and fourteen were six times more likely to be dependent on inhalants than those who did not use inhalants until they were between fifteen and seventeen years of age.

The NSDUH survey found that in 2007, approximately 663,000 youths aged twelve or thirteen had used inhalants at least once in their lifetime. The most often used inhalants were glue, shoe polish, toluene, gasoline or lighter fluid, and spray paints.

The Youth Risk Behavior Surveillance System, conducted by the U.S. Centers for Disease Control and Prevention (CDC) in 2009, found that for grades 9 through 12, inhalant use levels decreased from 20.3 percent in 1995 to 11.7 percent in 2009.

The 2005 NSDUH also reports a connection between the abuse of inhalants and participation in other

The Very Youngest Users

In the United States, formal research studies list ages twelve to thirteen as the youngest age range for inhalant abuse. However, there are reports of children as young as four and five abusing inhalants.

One of the scariest facts about inhalants is the age at which most people first experiment with them. The average age of initial use is ten, about a year and a half before the average person tries cigarettes.

Inhalants and Solvents—Sniffing Disaster

Percentages of Youths Aged 12 or 13 Reporting Lifetime Use of Inhalants, by Inhalant Type: 2002 and 2003

Substance	Percentage
glue, shoe polish or toluene	4.3
gasoline or lighter fluid	3.3
spray paints	2.9
correction fluid, degreaser, or cleaning fluid	2.1
lacquer thinner or other paint solvents	1.4
other aerosol sprays	1.3
amyl nitrite, "poppers," locker-room odorizers, or "rush"	1.2
lighter gases (butane, propane)	1.1
nitrous oxide or whippets	0.3
halothane, ether, or other anesthetics	0.3

(*Source*: The NSDUH Report, March 17, 2005.)

delinquent behaviors. Youths aged twelve or thirteen who abused inhalants were more likely to participate in other delinquent activities than were their peers who were not inhalant abusers. Youths in this age cohort who had used inhalants in their lifetime were more than twice as likely to have been in a serious fight at school or work in the past year than youths who had never abused the substances. When it came to theft, the individuals who had abused inhalants were six times as likely to have stolen, or had attempted to steal something worth more than fifty dollars. Just over 35 percent of youths aged twelve or thirteen who had used inhalants at some point in their lifetime had experimented with other illegal drugs.

Inhalant abuse can signal a lifetime of difficulty. Although inhalant abuse is still low (more than 86 percent of adults between the ages of eighteen and forty-nine indicated they had never used inhalants during their lifetime), those who began abusing inhalants at age thirteen or below were more likely to have some problems not reported by individuals who began their abuse at age fourteen or older. Those who began using inhalants before age fourteen, for example, were more likely to have abused alcohol or illegal drugs during the previous twelve months.

In Canada, *epidemiological* data is not compiled on inhalant abuse. However, *anecdotal* evidence finds that inhalant abuse there is not dissimilar to that in the United States. Inhalant abuse has been reported in children as young as six to eight years old. Most inhalant abuse occurs between the ages of fourteen and fifteen. By the time the person reaches nineteen, the abuse has generally tapered off until it ends. However, some individu-

Percentages of Youths Aged 12 or 13 Who Participated in Delinquent Behaviors One or More Times in the Past Year, by Lifetime Inhalant Use: 2002 and 2003

Behavior	User	Nonuser
serious fight at school or work	45.0	20.3
group-against-group fight	38.7	15.0
attacked with intent to seriously hurt	20.2	5.6
stole or tried to steal anything worth more than $50	10.2	1.7
sold illegal drugs	3.2	0.6
carried a handgun	7.6	2.1

(*Source:* The NSDUH Report, March 17, 2005.)

Results from the 2011 NSDUH survey indicate:

• 1.1% of the US population currently uses inhalants
• 1.4% of youths between 12 and 13 use inhalants
• the percentage of youths who used inhalants dropped as age increased
• 9.0% of drug users said their first drug had been inhalants
• 793,009 people had used inhalants for the first time in the past 12 months

Studies have shown that inhalant abuse begins even before the onset of alcohol and tobacco abuse. One reason for this may be that many inhalants are found in common household products.

als do continue to abuse inhalants into their adulthood. For both countries, the reasons individuals begin to abuse inhalants are similar.

Who Abuses Inhalants?

Although there is not just one profile of the individual who abuses inhalants, it is true that most of the individuals who abuse inhalants are white. Males still outnumber females abusing inhalants, but the girls are quickly closing in; chronic inhalant abuse, however, is still dominated by males. On their website www.inhalants.org/charac.htm, the National Inhalant Prevention Coalition lists some of the characteristics shared by many:

Age of Onset
- Often first substance used before marijuana and cocaine. In fact, inhalant use often appears before onset of tobacco or alcohol use.
- Experimental use onset occurs in late childhood and early adolescence, and use patterns are short lived, with cessation in late adolescence.
- Chronic use appears in early and late adolescence.

Fast and Multiple Intoxication
- Users can get high several times over a short period because inhalants are short-acting with a rapid onset.
- This quality is attractive to children who don't like delayed gratification.

Poor School Attendance
- drop-outs
- absenteeism
- suspension
- expulsion

Delinquency
- particularly theft and burglary
- Inhalant users are more disruptive, deviant, or delinquent than other drug users.

Ethnic Membership
- Users are predominately white.
- Minority involvement is concentrated in American and Canadian Native American Indians, and low-income Hispanics.

Gender
- Experimental use equally common in males, females.
- Chronic use most common in males.

Males are more likely than females to chronically abuse inhalants. This can lead to emotional problems, such as anxiety, depression and anger.

- Morbidity and mortality more common among chronic male users.
- some male homosexuals (limited to nitrites)

High-Exposure Occupational Settings
- adults in certain high-exposure occupational settings (e.g., painters)

High-Exposure Professions
- adult medical workers (e.g., anesthesiologist, dentist)

Use of Multiple Inhalants
- Exposure to solvent mixtures either in occupational or abuse settings is far more common than exposure to a single solvent.

Use of Other Drugs

Multiple Personal and Social Problems

Poor Adjustment to Work Environments

Multiproblem and Disrupted Families

Varied Socioeconomic Conditions
- impoverished, marginal, or ghetto situations
- middle to upper income

Parental Alcohol/Drug Abuse

Weakened Parental Influence
- Some parents do not discourage their child's use of inhalants.
- Some parents have low sanctions against inhalant use by peers of their children.

Poor School Performance and Adjustment
- attention deficit; poor short-term memory
- low abstraction and judgment scores
- lower grades

Lower Intelligence Scores (verbal and performance)

Psychopathology
- Users seeking treatment have high rates of psychopathology, especially conduct disorders and personality disorders.

- More psychopathology in those who use when they are alone.
- antisocial personality
- depressive disorder

Emotional Problems
- More emotional problems occur than among other drug users or non-drug users (especially anxiety, depression, and anger).

Weak or Negative Future Orientations
- Users have dismal or no future orientations; uncertain whether or not the future is worth waiting for.

Low Self-Esteem

High Adolescent Rebellion

Strong Peer Drug Influence
- Peers have high inhalant and drug use.
- Peers have high deviance behaviors.
- Peer cluster theory indicates that inhalant use is apt to occur in groups of teens.

Special Setting
- prisons
- boarding schools

Acculturation Stress

Criminal Justice System Involvement
- more family members in prison

Among ethnic groups, American Indian or Alaska Native and Hispanic Latino are most often abusers of inhalants. Those of Asian or Native Hawaiian or Other Pacific Islander descent are the least likely to abuse inhalants; this is true with other illegal or illicit substances as well.

In another attempt to understand who abuses inhalants, and why, with the ultimate goal of helping those

Peer influence is a powerful force in adolescents' lives. Sometimes this influence can be positive or harmless—but if an adolescents' friends use inhalants or other drugs, she will be more likely to try them as well.

Inhalants and Solvents—Sniffing Disaster

Inhalant abuse is higher among people suffering from poverty. This might be due to the fact that inhalants dull hunger and reduce the feeling of cold.

who are hooked on inhalants and to prevent others from developing an addiction to inhalants, doctors Neil Rosenberg and Charles Sharp (www.inhalants.org/guidelines.htm) developed a scale that categorizes abusers by their frequency of inhalant abuse:

- transient social user—short history of use, use with friends, average intelligence, ten to sixteen years old.
- chronic social user—long history of use (five or more years), daily use with friends, minor legal involvement, poor social skills, limited education, brain damage, twenty to thirty years old.
- transient isolate user—short history of use, solo use, ten to sixteen years old.
- chronic isolate user—long history of use (five or more years), daily solo use, legal involvement, poor social skills, limited education, brain damage, twenty to twenty-nine years old.

Why Inhalants?

There are a lot of substances that are available for abuse, so why does someone choose to abuse inhalants? According to the National Inhalant Prevention Coalition (http://www.inhalants.org), some of the reasons adolescents give for abusing inhalants are:

- experimentation
- peer group pressure
- cost effectiveness
- easy availability
- convenient packaging ("It can be easily hidden in my pocket.")
- the course of intoxication ("It's a quicker drunk.")

- the "high" doesn't last too long
- the hangover is usually less severe than what is found in alcohol

Of those reasons, perhaps the main reason inhalants are attractive to those inclined toward substance abuse is their availability. It's probably safe to say that every home in North America (well, at least most) contains some source of inhalant or solvent. Schools and offices have inhalants and solvents as well. For the individual looking to abuse a substance, inhalants and solvents offer him or her a **veritable** smorgasbord from which to choose.

Even if someone doesn't have inhalants and solvents available at home, school, or office, it is easy enough to get them. The most popular inhalants can be legitimately purchased at almost any grocery store, pharmacy, or office supply store. There are no age requirements or limits on the amount that can be purchased in most cases.

Separation from family also plays a role in who develops problems with inhalant abuse. The 2004 NSDUH found that adolescents who had spent time in the foster-care system were almost five times more likely to develop a dependence on inhalants that individuals who were never placed in foster care.

The National Inhalant Prevention Coalition also found that poverty plays a role in inhalant abuse, but perhaps not in a way most might think. Yes, inhalants are inexpensive compared to other illegal or illicit drugs, and that is certainly a factor for their abuse among low-income groups. Perhaps more significant for those in this population group, however, inhalants also help **mitigate** some of the physical effects of poverty; inhalants can dull the pain of hunger as well as buffer the feeling of being cold. This aspect of inhalant abuse

Inhalant abuse is high among the Native American and Hispanic American populations. Gasoline is the most commonly abused inhalant; sometimes inhaled directly from a recently used pump nozzle.

Inhalants and Solvents—Sniffing Disaster

may play a part in its proliferation among Native and Hispanic populations.

Inhalant Abuse Among Indigenous and Hispanic Populations

When it comes to substance abuse in the United States, members of the Native American and Hispanic American populations hold a dubious distinction: individuals from these two groups generally make up the largest proportion of minority abusers. This is also true for inhalant abuse. According to the 2007 NSDUH Report, 9.3 percent of the U.S. population age twelve or older surveyed indi-

Who Uses Inhalants?

Inhalants are abused throughout the United States. According to the National Drug Intelligence Center, in 11 states the percentage of high school students who reported having used inhalants at least once in their lifetime exceeded the national average of 14.6 percent. The states having the highest percentage of inhalant abuse are West Virginia (20.4%), Tennessee (19.2%), Nevada (19.0%), Wyoming (17.6%), Ohio (17.1%), Arkansas (16.7%), Montana (16.5%), Wisconsin (16.2%), Alabama (16.1%), Michigan (15.6%), and North Dakota (15.5%).

While adolescents are the primary group abusing inhalants, a study by the Texas Commission on Alcohol and Drug Abuse (TCADA) found that adults also abuse inhalants. An analysis of 144 Texas death certificates involving misuse or abuse of inhalants indicates that the average age of those who suffered inhalant deaths was 25.6 with ages ranging from 8 to 62. In the same analysis of Texas death certificates, TCADA found that the most frequently mentioned inhalant (35%) was Freon (51 deaths). Of the Freon deaths, 42 percent were students or youth (mean age of 16.4 years), and 37 percent were involved in occupations where Freon was readily available.

The village of Sheshatshiu has a very serious addiction problem. Many of the Innu children leave home and turn to inhalants because their parents are alcoholics.

Inhalants and Solvents—Sniffing Disaster

Inhalants are dangerous not only because of how they affect the body, but because many of them are highly flammable. Lighting a match in the vicinity of inhalants could prove deadly.

cated that they had used inhalants during their lifetimes. Of that number, 12.8 percent were American Indian or Alaska Native; 7.1 percent were Hispanic or Latino. The percentage of Native American Indian or Alaska Native who used inhalants during their lifetime increases (to 18.4 percent) when the age surveyed changes to eighteen to twenty-five, but so does the total population percentage (to 12.5 percent). In 2006, the most prevalent use of inhalants occurs between the ages of eighteen to twenty-five. This is a shift from the 2005 survey, in which the highest use was between the ages twelve to seventeen.

Things are not that different in Canada. As in the United States, inhalant abuse in Canada crosses all ethnic boundaries. It is most prevalent in the First Nations population, members of government-recognized **Aboriginal** groups. An ongoing study of students in Ontario, conducted by Canada's Centre for Addiction and Mental Health (CAMH), found that use of inhalants by adolescents increased from 2.6 percent in 1997 to 7.3 percent in 1999. From 1999 to 2001, however, use by adolescents decreased to 5.9 percent. In 2011, use was 5.6 percent.

In both the Native populations and among Hispanic Americans, gasoline is the inhalant of choice. In some cases, they siphon the gas from vehicles. At other times, they simply haunt gas stations, taking big sniffs from recently used pump nozzles.

The reasons for abuse among **indigenous** and Hispanic American populations are hypothesized to be similar to the "whys" listed earlier in this chapter. Poverty, peer pressure, and perceived lack of opportunity may play larger roles among members of this group, as evidenced in the story of one First Nations group with a very large problem with inhalant abuse.

What to Do When Someone Is Huffing

- Remain calm and do not panic.
- Do not excite or argue with the abuser when they are under the influence, as they can become aggressive or violent.
- If the person is unconscious or not breathing, call for help. CPR should be administered until help arrives.
- If the person is conscious, keep him or her calm and in a well-ventilated room.
- Excitement or stimulation can cause hallucinations or violence.
- Activity or stress may cause heart problems, which may lead to "Sudden Sniffing Death."
- Talk with other persons present or check the area for clues to what was used.
- Once the person is recovered, seek professional help for the abuser: school nurse, counselor, physician, other health care worker.
- If use is suspected, adults should be frank but not accusatory in discussions with youth about potential inhalant use.

(*Source*: National Inhalant Prevention Coalition. www.inhalants.org/whatodo.htm.)

The Innu of Sheshatshiu

In a small village located on the coast of Labrador in Canada, substance abuse—including inhalants—is taking its toll on the Innu population. The Innu (which in their native language means "human being) is one of that country's Aboriginal peoples. It was also one of the last groups to turn to village life, not doing so until the 1960s. Before then, the Innu relied on hunting and led a more nomadic life. From its discovery by Europeans in the eighteenth century until the 1930s, the village of Sheshatshiu and its people played an important role in the fur-trade industry, some experts claiming the village and its people were too dependent on the fur industry. And they were probably right. In the 1930s, during the early years of the **Great Depression**, the bottom fell out of the fur industry. With millions worldwide jobless, people formed lines to get bread and food—not furs. What had once been their bread-and-butter industry was now almost nonexistent for the Innu and Sheshatshiu.

As if that wasn't enough of a blow to the small village, the caribou population suffered a severe downsizing during the same time. Again, the village and its people found themselves without a potential money source, as well as food source. The trouble didn't end there, either. The provincial government placed hunting restrictions on the Innu, and in the 1970s, much of the Innu land, including land used for hunting, was flooded to make way for a hydroelectric project. Environmental concerns have delayed plans for development of a nickel mine in the area.

Today, Sheshatshiu has about 1,600 residents, most of them Innu, and a serious problem with substance abuse. Though many of the adults in the village have alcohol abuse problems, many of its children have fallen victim to inhalant abuse. According to Chief Paul Rich, gas sniffing has become an overwhelming force in the lives of many of the village's children. One of the adolescents is quoted on the website of CBC News (www.cbc.ca/news/background/aboriginals/sheshatshiu.html):

> My name is Phillip. I'm a gas sniffer. I sniff gas with my friends. . . . They haven't been home in days. They sniff around the clock and, like the others, pass out in a shelter—their only glimmer of stability, only source of food in an otherwise chaotic existence. For them, out here, in the freezing cold, is

better than home. I don't go home because I sniff gas. And I sniff gas because both of my parents are drinking and I'm mad at that. And the other reason is they can't afford to buy me what I need.

Poverty and peer pressure certainly play roles in the inhalant abuse problem of the Innu of Sheshatshiu. So do memories. In the spring of 2004, eleven-year-old Charles Rich was playing with a candle in a friend's basement. Although that was risky enough, Charles was also bagging at the same time, which created a deadly combination. When the candle caused the bag to catch fire, the deadly flames ignited Charles. His brothers Carl and Phillip watched Charles—ablaze—run for help, making the fire spread more. Charles was burned over more than 80 percent of his body. Now, Carl, Phillip, and their sister Angela sniff to be close to the sibling lost to inhalants. "Charles tries to get me to stop. I won't stop because it's the only way I can communicate with Charles," Carl is quoted as saying on the CBC website. Angela concurs: "I can't and I won't stop sniffing gas because when I do, I see my brother."

The village chief, Paul Rich (who is not related to the Rich children), knows that fighting inhalant abuse is an uphill battle with no end in sight. He acknowledges that part of the problem is an adult population with a serious alcoholism problem. The economic problems of the past and present have left many Innu feeling hopeless. "They feel hopeless because there's nothing out there that gives them the incentive to stop drinking. Sometimes when that happens, the parents forget about their kids."

Like many families in Sheshatshiu, the Rich children are growing up with alcoholic parents. Carl, Phillip, and

Angela have even tried bargaining with their parents to get them to stop drinking. Though their parents did stop drinking, the children didn't stop sniffing. And their parents didn't stay alcohol free for long. Louison Rich, the children's mother, laments:

> "This is how we grew up, all our relatives drank. Nobody taught us how to drink . . . same thing with our children. We didn't teach them how to sniff. Maybe we have similar cases, their sniffing and our drinking. They see us drink and they sniff."

And the cycle continues.

Will things get better for the Innu of Sheshatshiu? Perhaps, but probably not immediately. In 2002, they were recognized by the government as a First Nations group. This makes them eligible for government benefits, and gives them more input over such basic things as education, health care, or social services. New schools and health care centers have been built. It may also help more inhalant-abusing adolescents get treatment in nearby Goose Bay. In the past, adolescents were forcibly removed when their parents refused to get help for them. And then, there are children like Angela:

> "I think I'll never stop sniffing gas. I want the same thing to happen to me that happened to my brother Charles. I want to die the same way my brother died . . . while sniffing gas."

Without treatment, Angela may get her wish. It's still a very real possibility for Angela and many others of Sheshatshiu.

Inhalants and Solvents—Sniffing Disaster

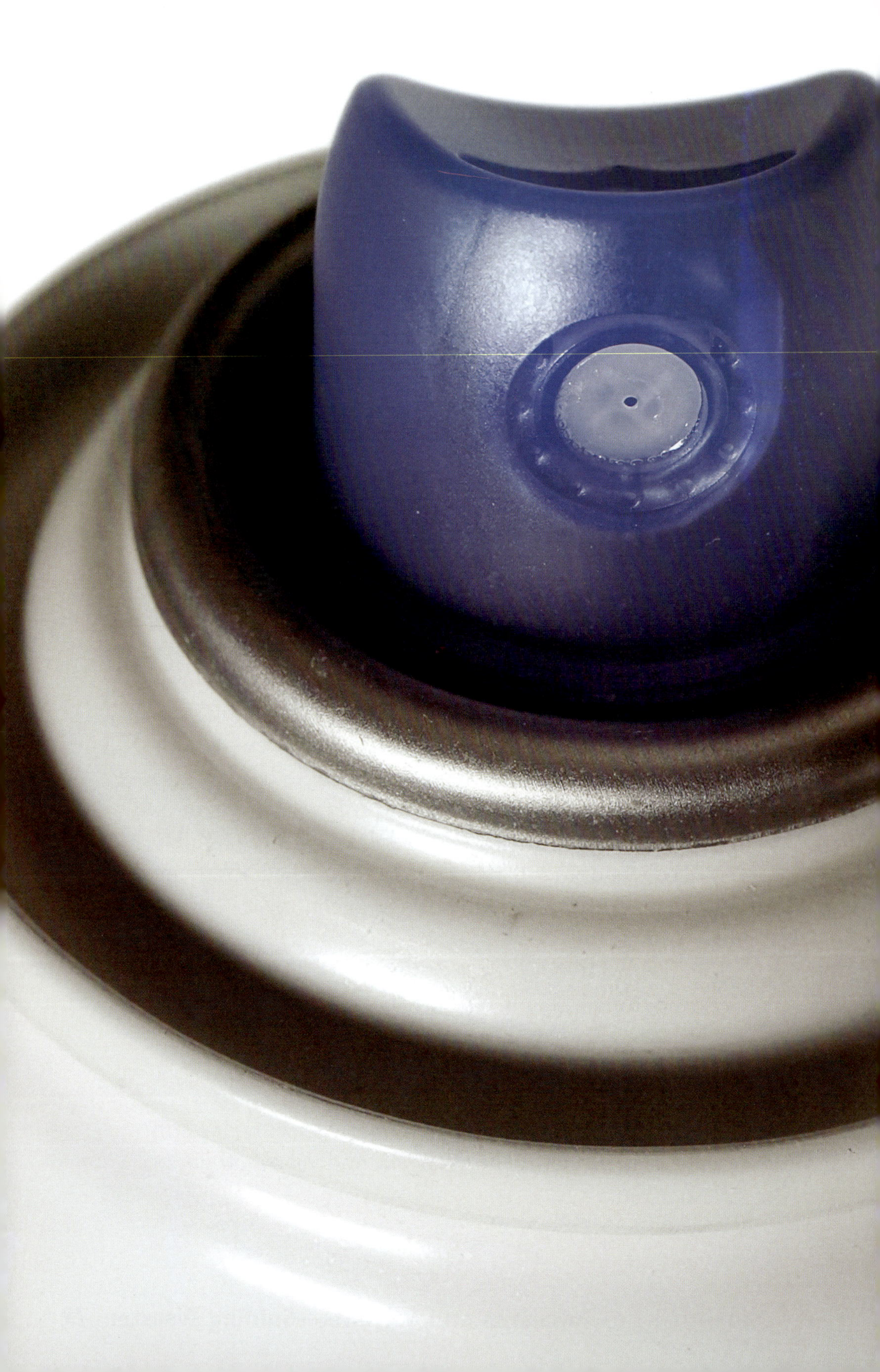

4 Treatment for Inhalant and Solvent Addiction

On March 25, at 10:30 p.m., we received a call from the hospital telling us that Jeny had been in an accident. They wouldn't tell me she was okay, just to get to the hospital. After driving for 15 minutes to get there, we weren't allowed to see her and couldn't find out if she was okay. We waited two hours before a police officer took us to another room. He showed us a cleaning product. He said the driver of the car had "huffed" it.

We had no idea of what he was talking about—never heard of huffing. The driver of the car had inhaled the cleaner and immediately passed out. The car went down an embankment, across interstate 75 and hit the cement divider in the medium.

Very few people die from using inhalants, but some do. And, using inhalants while driving may result in the deaths of other people as well.

The driver and the two passengers in the backseat walked away. Jeny's head went through the windshield and hit the divider. She died immediately.

Jeny was an A-B student, popular in her school, loved life—and I know she would have never tried inhalants had she known the danger and especially riding with someone who was driving and inhaling. They were "just having fun." We never got to say goodbye to Jeny. In a matter of minutes, her life was cruelly taken away. So, for the parents reading this, please know what your child is doing, . . . For the kids out there reading this, please don't be stupid.

Don't think inhalants can't hurt you, because they can and they kill. Don't allow your parents to go through the nightmare we are now living.

(Source: Alliance for Consumer Education.)

It's true. Most people who abuse inhalants do not die because of it. But, some do, and some may not die themselves, but are responsible for the deaths of others, such as Jeny. Beating an addiction to anything—alcohol, cocaine, gambling—is hard work. Kicking the inhalant habit may be harder than most.

First a word about terminology. Although sometimes used interchangeably, addiction and dependence are not the same things. When someone is dependent on a substance, the body needs that substance in order to function. Addiction is a psychological dependency on the substance. If someone is dependent on a substance, that does not always mean the person is or will become addicted to the substance.

Detoxification

Some experts call inhalation abusers a "hidden population." Generally, individuals who abuse inhalants aren't making drug deals on the street or buying and hiding drug paraphernalia such as syringes or pipes. No, inhalant abusers can just go to the kitchen cabinet and get what they need. Because of the availability of the inhalants and the simplicity of their intake, this abuse often goes undetected until the user gets caught or decides on his own to kick the inhalant habit. When that happens, inhalant abusers may go through withdrawal symptoms.

When the body gets used to having a certain substance and that substance becomes unavailable, the body can "object." For example, take someone who has had coffee or other caffeinated beverages several times a day, but then decides to cut it out "cold turkey." She might find herself suffering from extreme headaches and perhaps be a bit jittery. Her body is going through withdrawal—experiencing symptoms of not having the caffeine it has been used to having in its system.

In the case of inhalants, withdrawal symptoms are usually minor, such as hand tremors, headaches, nervousness, or excessive sweating. Sometimes, however, the withdrawal symptoms are more serious as the body goes through the detoxification process. When one decides to break free from addiction, the body goes through this detoxification process to rid itself of the drug's toxic substances. During detoxification, the body goes through withdrawal symptoms as the toxins are eliminated from the system. More severe inhalant withdrawal symptoms can include:

- sleep disturbance
- irritability

Inhalant abuse can often go undetected for a long time. This is because the user can just reach into the kitchen cabinet to get her supplies, rather than needing any special dealers or paraphernalia.

Inhalants and Solvents—Sniffing Disaster

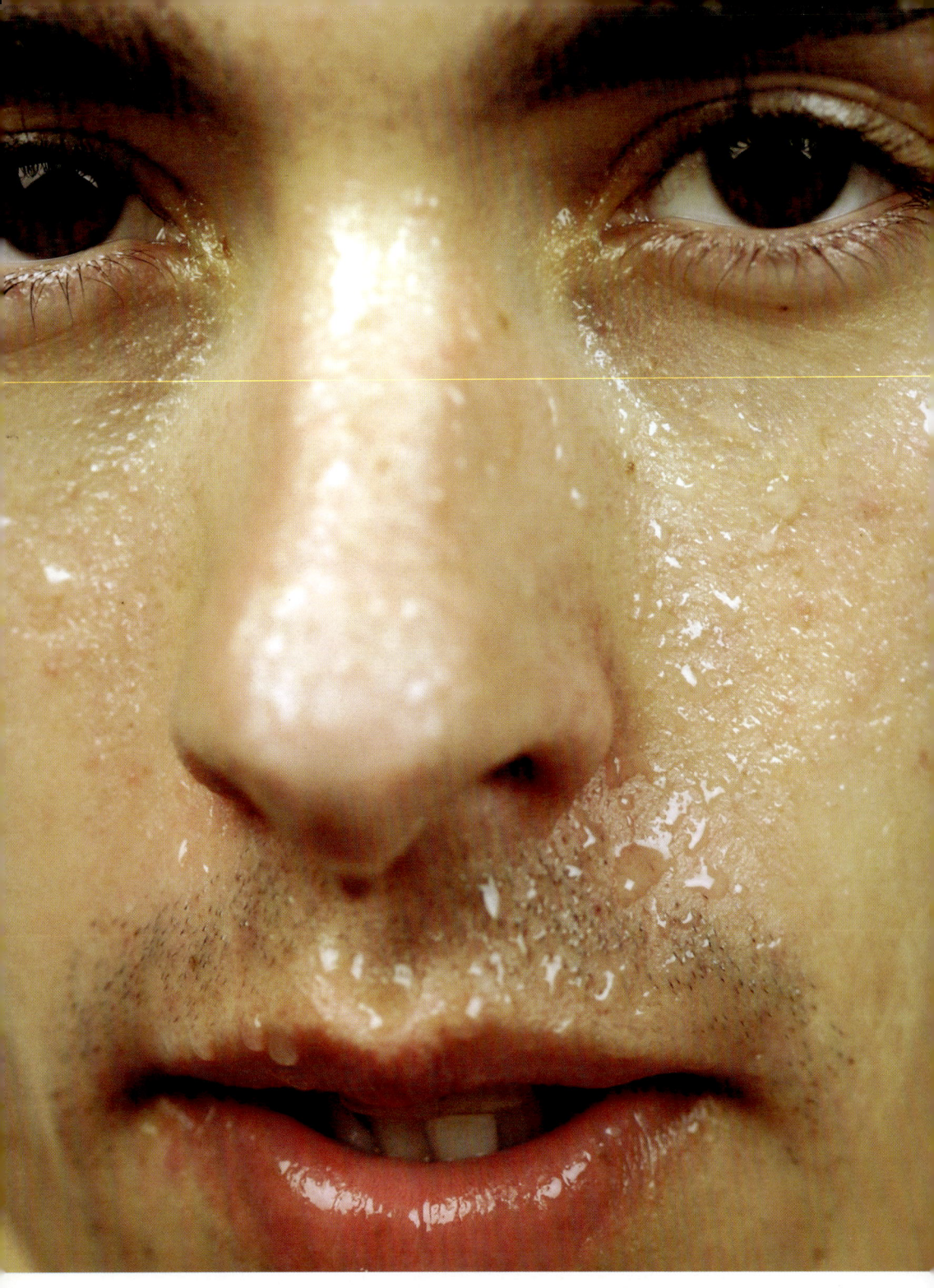

Withdrawal symptoms occur when the body is ridding itself of a drug's toxic substances. In the case of inhalants, these symptoms are usually mild and include headaches and excessive sweating.

82 Chapter 4—Treatment for Inhalant and Solvent Addiction

- jitteriness
- *diaphoresis*
- nausea and vomiting
- *tachycardia*
- hallucinations or *delusions*

Detoxification from inhalants does not take place overnight. Some of the toxins contained in inhalants remain in the body for a long time, some for a month or more. There is also a high incidence of relapse during the withdrawal phase.

Although there are some characteristics of inhalant abuse that lend themselves to traditional treatment methods, other aspects of this addiction are not **conducive** to programs with proven *efficacy*. In fact, because of the high relapse rates and the perceived unlikelihood of success, many treatment programs will not admit individuals trying to reach sobriety from inhalant abuse.

Treatment Programs

For some drug addictions, the detoxification process might be enough to prevent further use. This is especially true if the habit was short lived or the dosage small. But, for the individual with a habit of inhalant abuse, this is not likely to be the case. For people who have abused inhalants or for those with chronic or long-term addictions to other drugs, follow-up care is necessary; in the case of inhalant abuse, treatment can last for two years. Studies have shown that most people with addictions will return to their previous behaviors if treatment ends with detoxification. Participation in a formal treatment program can make the difference between success and failure.

The NIDA has come up with a list of thirteen principles that make up a good treatment program. These include:

1. *No single treatment is appropriate for all individuals.* Matching treatment settings, interventions, and services to each individual's particular problems and needs is critical to his or her ultimate success in returning to productive functioning in the family, workplace, and society.

2. *Treatment needs to be readily available.* Because individuals who are addicted to drugs may be uncertain about entering treatment, taking advantage of opportunities when they are ready for treatment is crucial. Potential treatment applicants can be lost if treatment is not immediately available or is not readily accessible.

3. *Effective treatment attends to multiple needs of the individual, not just his or her drug use.* To be effective, treatment must address the individual's drug use and any associated medical, psychological, social, vocational, and legal problems.

4. *An individual's treatment and services plan must be assessed continually and modified as necessary to ensure that the plan meets the person's changing needs.* A patient may require varying combinations of services and treatment components during the course of treatment and recovery. In addition to counseling or psychotherapy, a patient at times may require medication, other medical services, family therapy, parenting instruction, vocational rehabilitation, and social and legal services. It is critical that the treatment

The end of withdrawal symptoms marks the end of physical dependence on a drug. However, further treatment must continue to help the individual recover from the psychological need.

approach be appropriate to the individual's age, gender, ethnicity, and culture.

5. *Remaining in treatment for an adequate period of time is critical for treatment effectiveness.* The appropriate duration for an individual depends on his or her problems and needs. Research indicates that for most patients, the threshold of significant improvement is reached at about three months in treatment. After this threshold is reached, additional treatment can produce further progress toward recovery. Because people often leave treatment prematurely, programs should include strategies to engage and keep patients in treatment.

A person going through treatment for drug addiction needs a program that can adjust to her changing needs. Therefore, the treatment plan needs to be continually assessed and modified if necessary.

86 Chapter 4—Treatment for Inhalant and Solvent Addiction

6. *Counseling (individual and/or group) and other behavioral therapies are critical components of effective treatment for addiction.* In therapy, patients address issues of motivation, build skills to resist drug use, replace drug-using activities with constructive and rewarding nondrug-using activities, and improve problem-solving abilities. Behavioral therapy also facilitates interpersonal relationships and the individual's ability to function in the family and community.

7. *Medications are an important element of treatment for many patients, especially when combined with counseling and other behavioral therapies.* For patients with mental disorders who have used an illegal drug to self-medicate, both behavioral treatments and medications can be critically important.

8. *Addicted or drug-abusing individuals with coexisting mental disorders should have both disorders treated in an integrated way.* Because addictive disorders and mental disorders often occur in the same individual, patients presenting for either condition should be assessed and treated for the co-occurrence of the other type of disorder.

9. *Medical detoxification is only the first stage of addiction treatment and by itself does little to change long-term drug use.* Medical detoxification safely manages the acute physical symptoms of withdrawal associated with stopping drug use. While detoxification alone is rarely sufficient to help addicts achieve long-term abstinence, for some individuals it is a strongly indicated precursor to effective drug addiction treatment.

10. *Treatment does not need to be voluntary to be effective.* Strong motivation can facilitate the treatment process, however. Sanctions or enticements in the family, employment setting, or criminal justice system can increase significantly both treatment entry and retention rates and the success of drug treatment interventions.

11. *Possible drug use during treatment must be monitored continuously.* Lapses to drug use can occur during treatment. The objective monitoring of a patient's drug and alcohol use during treatment, such as through urinalysis or other tests, can help the patient withstand urges to use drugs. Such monitoring also can provide early evidence of drug use so that the individual's treatment plan can be adjusted. Feedback to patients who test positive for illicit drug use is an important element of monitoring.

12. *Treatment programs should provide assessment for HIV/AIDS, hepatitis B and C, tuberculosis and other infectious diseases, and counseling to help patients modify or change behaviors that place themselves or others at risk of infection.* Counseling can help patients avoid high-risk behavior. Counseling also can help people who are already infected manage their illness.

13. *Recovery from drug addiction can be a long-term process and frequently requires multiple episodes of treatment.* As with other chronic illnesses, relapses to drug use can occur during or after successful treatment episodes. Addicted individuals may require prolonged treatment and multiple episodes of treatment to achieve

long-term abstinence and fully restored functioning. Participation in self-help support programs during and following treatment often is helpful in maintaining abstinence.

For most drug problems, there are two primary treatment methods: behavioral and **pharmacological**.

Behavioral Treatment Programs

Put simply, behavioral treatment programs teach people with addictions to change their behaviors so they are less likely to repeat those that led to addiction in the first place. But, nothing about addiction is simple. Though behavioral treatment programs do help those with addictions find ways to avoid behaviors that can cause a relapse, they also help them to discover what led to those behaviors initially. Cognitive-behavioral therapy helps the individuals recognize how thought patterns influence behaviors. With therapy, individuals learn how to change negative thought patterns, thereby changing behaviors. Individual and family therapy can help the person with addiction and those around her learn how to live with and as a recovering addict. Therapy can also help the addicted individual and her associates handle relapses, since most people, including those fighting inhalant abuse, do relapse at some point during recovery.

Behavioral treatment programs also help those with addictions handle life without the drugs being abused, including sometimes painful cravings for the substance. The individual must also learn how to deal with having most of these substances around them every day. The best treatment results are achieved when the individual practices **abstinence** from all drugs.

Behavioral treatment programs often begin with a period of inpatient treatment. Depending on the length, severity, and drug of addiction, inpatient treatment can be short term (usually a minimum of thirty days) or long-term residential. At first, some programs allow inpatients to have minimal—if any—contact with the "outside world." They concentrate on learning about themselves and their relationship with the drug. Later, family and perhaps close friends are encouraged to participate in the treatment program.

Pharmacological Treatment Programs

Medications have proven to be effective in treating addiction to many substances. They are used in both inpatient and outpatient settings. There are medications available that can aid in the treatment of many addictions.

Most treatment programs use a combination of behavioral and pharmacological methods in helping someone find and live a life of sobriety. Many treatment programs also encourage their clients to supplement their programs with support groups such as Narcotics Anonymous.

Narcotics Anonymous

Based on the twelve-step program Alcoholics Anonymous (AA), Narcotics Anonymous (NA) helps those addicted to prescription painkillers stay sober in the outside world. The first NA meetings were held in the early 1950s in Los Angeles, California. As found on its website (www.na.org), the organization described itself this way in its first publication:

> NA is a nonprofit fellowship or society of men and women for whom drugs had become a major prob-

Treatment does not have to be voluntary to be effective. However, if an individual is sentenced to treatment by the criminal justice system, some motivation will help with the treatment process.

lem. We . . . meet regularly to help each other stay clean. . . . We are not interested in what or how much you used . . . but only in what you want to do about your problem and how we can help.

In the more than fifty years since, it has grown into one of the largest organizations of its kind. Today, groups are located all over the world, and its books and pamphlets are published in thirty-two languages. No matter where the group is located, each chapter is based on the twelve steps first formulated in AA:

1. We admitted we were powerless over drugs—that our lives had become unmanageable.
2. Came to believe that a Power greater than ourselves could restore us to sanity.

Behavioral treatment teaches a person with an addiction to understand the behaviors that led to her addiction so she can avoid those behaviors in the future. It will also be important to learn how to practice abstinence from all drugs, even if the substances are around her every day.

3. Made a decision to turn our will and our lives over to the care of God as we understand Him.
4. Made a searching and fearless moral inventory of ourselves.
5. Admitted to God, and to our selves, and to another human being the exact nature of our wrongs.
6. We're entirely ready to have God remove all these defects of character.
7. Humbly asked Him to remove our shortcomings.
8. Made a list of all persons we had harmed, and became willing to make amends to them all.
9. Made direct amends to such people wherever possible, except when to do so would injure them or others.

10. Continued to take personal inventory and when we were wrong promptly admitted it.
11. Sought through prayer and meditation to improve our conscious contact with God as we understand Him, praying only for knowledge of His will for us and the power to carry that out.
12. Having had a spiritual awakening as the result of these steps, we tried to carry this message to drug addicts and to practice these principles in all our affairs.

Though attendance at and participation in NA meetings will not guarantee a recovery free from temptation and relapse, they can play an important role in staying sober.

Treating Inhalant Abuse

While the success of these programs in the treatment of drug addiction cannot be discounted, they are ineffective for most individuals who are addicted to inhalants. The National Inhalant Prevention Coalition lists on its website (www.inhalants.org/guidelines.htm) reasons why traditional treatment programs might not be effective for those who have abused inhalants:

- detoxification from poisonous chemicals must be accomplished prior to planning for treatment
- detoxification and treatment cannot be accomplished within a 14 day, 21 day, or 28 day model; providing for an extended length of stay, allowing for a minimum patient stay of 90 days that can be extended to 120, would be most beneficial for the patient

- "talk therapy" may not be appropriate for persons with neurological and/or cognitive dysfunction
- short attention span, poor impulse control and/or poor social skills not appropriate for group therapy
- group therapy may not be appropriate initially, as users of alcohol and other drugs often reject or are **contemptuous** of inhalant abusers
- **neurocognitive** damage may impair decision-making skills

It is necessary for these individuals, their families and health-care professionals to find alternative methods of treatment.

As mentioned earlier in this chapter, many treatment programs do not accept inhalant abusers. The chance of relapse and treatment failure makes the risk higher than many treatment facilities want to deal with. In those programs that do admit inhalant abusers, individuals should be aware that recovery is apt to be very slow going, with many peaks and valleys. Perhaps more than many substance abusers, individuals who abuse inhalants come to treatment with a lot of "baggage" that complicates treatment. They come with a **plethora** of social, physical, and intellectual problems.

A major consideration in the treatment of inhalation abuse is the age of the individual in treatment. Methods that are successful in treating sixteen- or seventeen-year-olds probably aren't going to work for a thirteen-year-old, the youngest age at which many experts feel treatment can be effective. Their youth and the immaturity of that age as well as that caused by drug abuse can make treatment very challenging for the staff of the treatment program and for the teen.

On admission, many undergoing treatment for inhalant abuse may be hesitant to work with adult counselors. Often this is a trust issue. Remember the description of inhalant abusers in chapter 3? The lack of a supportive family—or understanding adults in general—was one factor that led many down the inhalant abuse path in the first place. No matter how well meaning they might be, adults may not be the most effective teachers during the initial days at the treatment center.

Some treatment programs have found effective teachers for the newly admitted abusers of inhalants—those who have been in treatment for a while. Peer counselors or mentors can help the "newbie" feel more comfortable in what can be a stressful setting. They can show the new

One of the 12 steps in the Narcotics Anonymous program is to acknowledge that there is help to be found from a higher power.

person the ropes, and help her learn what to expect from the program and from the recovery process. Adults should not abdicate their responsibility however. Professionals must keep in mind that the veteran resident is still in treatment, still learning the hows and whys of their abuse and the skills necessary to live as a recovering substance abuser. It must always be at the forefront of the professionals' mind that relapse is a common occurrence, and that includes relapse by someone who has been in the program for a while. Also, individuals who have abused inhalants may have impaired decision-making skills, making it easy for them to make bad decisions when presented by peers. Peer counselors can help in the recovery process, but they should not be encouraged or allowed to be the primary force in the treatment program.

Chronic or long-term inhalant abuse can dramatically impair the ability of the abuser to live in the everyday world. Serious cognitive deficits brought on by inhalant abuse can make it difficult for individuals to learn new things or remember things they've already been taught. Though this is frustrating for the person in treatment and for those trying to help, it's a fact that just has to be considered in the scope of the treatment program.

Just as in other treatment programs for other addictions, family support is necessary to success. They must be made aware—as much as possible—of how the inhalant addiction developed, and their role in the process. Families need to receive education about inhalants and their dangers, and be willing to remove the products from their homes. Some will see life without inhalants and solvents as a major sacrifice. Treatment program staff should educate family members about alternatives to such products. Many aerosols, for example, now have a nonaerosol spray alternative.

Traditional forms of treatment are often ineffective for individuals addicted to inhalants. This is in part because of their cognitive dysfunction, short attention span and poor social skills.

Peer counselors and mentors have been found to be effective teachers for inhalant abusers newly admitted to treatment programs. However, professionals must still be a large part of the treatment process.

Both patients and their families need to go through an educational process. Many individuals thought that inhalants were not serious drugs. The fact that they are in treatment programs shows how mistaken they were. Families and patients should be educated about the dangers of inhalant abuse.

Again, one thing learned in all treatment programs is that recovery is an ongoing process; treatment doesn't end when the recovering addict walks out the door of the treatment center. This is especially true in inhalant abuse recovery, given that inhalants are readily available and the person in recovery may have cognitive difficulties and social skills still in need of polishing. In the case of children and adolescents who are in school, including the school counselor in the treatment plan has proven effective. It gives another layer of support to the individual seeking to live a sober life.

Pharmacology and Inhalant Abuse Treatment

The use of medication to treat addictions was discussed earlier in this chapter. This is yet another area in which treatment for inhalant addiction differs from that for other drugs. To ease withdrawal symptoms and to help control cravings, many treatment programs provide their clients with medications. For the individual who is undergoing treatment for inhalant addiction, that option is not available, at least for now.

A study conducted at the U.S. Department of Energy's Brookhaven Institute in 2004 has given some hope to those looking for pharmacological help in combating inhalant abuse. Scientists there found that vigabatrin (gamma vinyl-GABA, or GVG) might block the effects of toluene, an ingredient in many of the most-abused inhalants. When tested on animals that had been trained to look for toluene in certain areas, it was found that these animals did not spend as much time looking for the substance once they had received GVG. It is hoped that in humans, treatment with GVG would reduce, if not eliminate, the desire for toluene-containing substances.

Another Treatment Option

In Canada, the treatment of inhalant abuse among members of First Nations peoples is taking a more unique approach in the National Native Youth Solvent Addiction (NNYSA) program. This program emphasizes resiliency in the treatment of drug addiction.

As used by those involved with the NNYSA, resiliency is defined as the extent to which someone can recover from adversity. Stories of individuals who have come back from horrendous situations are well known, but what makes some individuals able to accomplish this and others to wallow in self-pity or even to become criminals? According to those responsible for the NNYSA, resiliency depends on risk and shield.

Risk consists of the adverse circumstances in which an individual lives. For example, some patients residing at the White Buffalo Youth Inhalant Treatment Centre had parents who were alcoholics and who suffered from physical and verbal abuse, multiple losses, and a lack of a support network.

The individual's strengths constitute the shields. These strengths include personal skills, spiritual beliefs and practices, and community supports. According to proponents of the risk and shield theory, shields come from qualities **inherent** in the individual or from community support and from adversity itself; they can be a result of facing difficult circumstances.

Treatment cannot end when the individual walks out the door of the treatment center. Recovery is an ongoing process; the individual will need the continuing support of his family, teachers and friends.

What Do Rehab Programs Accomplish?

Abstinence
In many cases it seems that as long as the substance is in the blood stream, thinking remains distorted. Often during the first days or weeks of total abstinence, we see a gradual clearing of thinking processes. This is a complex psychological and biological phenomenon, and is one of the elements that inpatient programs are able to provide by making sure the patient is fully detoxified and remains abstinent during his or her stay.

Removal of Denial
In some cases, when someone other than the patient, such as a parent, employer, or other authority, is convinced there is a problem, but the addict is not yet sure, voluntary attendance at a rehab program will provide enough clarification to remove this basic denial. Even those who are convinced they have a problem with substances usually don't admit to themselves or others the full extent of the addiction. Rehab uses group process to identify and help the individual to let go of these expectable forms of denial.

Removal of Isolation
As addictions progress, relationships deteriorate in quality. However, the bonds between fellow recovering people are widely recognized as one of the few forces powerful enough to keep recovery on track. The rehab experience, whether it is inpatient or outpatient, involves in-depth sharing in a group setting. This kind of sharing creates strong interpersonal bonds among group members. These bonds help to form a support system that will be powerful enough to sustain the individual during the first months of abstinence.

"Basic Training"
Basic training is a good way to think of the experience of rehab. Soldiers need a rapid course to give them the basic knowledge and skills they will need to fight in a war. Some kinds of learning need to be practiced so well that you can do them without thinking. In addition to the learning, trainees become physically fit, and perhaps most important, form emotional bonds that help keep up morale when the going is hard.

(*Source*: Partnership for a Drug-Free America)

The Native worldview places emphasis on one's spiritual self. They—and many non-Natives as well—believe that it is the strength, the shield, that is developed from the individual's spirit that helps one find the resiliency to rise above the bad, even to learn from it. The NNYSA treatment programs help individuals learn about their culturally based spirituality. The strength they learn to develop from their spiritual selves, combined with the shields they have inherently, can work together to help individuals achieve sobriety.

Aftercare

Substance abuse recovery is a process that takes time, patience, and hard work. Time spent as a resident in a treatment center is just one step toward achieving the goal of living a sober life. After leaving the treatment program, the recovering inhalant abuser needs the support of others to increase the possibility of success.

For some, in-person support groups are helpful. If possible, it is often best to find a group dealing with the same addiction, so that individuals can better relate to their common problems. If someone can't go to a group meeting or is too shy or otherwise uncomfortable sharing in person with a group, the Internet is full of chat rooms and e-mail lists that might be helpful. Though support groups can provide beneficial information and insight, it is important to keep in mind that the participants are not (in most cases, anyway) medical professionals. What has worked for one person may not work with another.

There is one truth that extends to all forms of substance abuse—the best way to treat abuse is to never begin taking the drug or substance at all. Prevention is the number-one cure.

no

5 It's More Than Just Say No

In 1980, First Lady Nancy Reagan first became aware of the extent of the drug abuse problem in the United States. With her backing, the Just Say No anti-drug advertising campaign geared up. During the 1980s and 1990s, Just Say No ads seemed to be everywhere. Just Say No rallies, bumper stickers, buttons, and other paraphernalia popped up. Britain even adopted the campaign in their fight against drugs.

Eventually, the Just Say No campaign became the subject of cartoons, jokes, and parodies. Although its real effectiveness is questionable, it was based on an undeniable truth—you can't become addicted if you don't use.

Legal Attempts at Prevention

Unlike cocaine, marijuana, and other such drugs, there are few restrictions on the purchase, possession, or use of

Controlled Substances Act

In 1970, the U.S. Congress enacted the Controlled Substances Act (CSA) as part of the Comprehensive Drug Abuse Prevention and Control Act, an attempt to deal with the country's drug problem. The CSA is the mechanism under which the federal government regulates the manufacture, importation, possession, and distribution of certain drugs.

The CSA also led to the creation of the five drug schedules used to classify drugs. Working together, the U.S. Department of Justice and the Department of Health and Human Services decide what drugs to include on the schedules based on their potential for abuse, accepted medical uses, and the potential for addiction.

inhalants. Some states, such as Arizona, have laws prohibiting the sale, transfer, or offer to sell to a minor any vapor-releasing substance that contains a toxin. In Connecticut, the sale or distribution to a minor of any product containing nitrous oxide is prohibited. The state of Idaho prohibits minors from possessing any aerosol product or other inhalant for the purposes of intoxication. Colorado and Florida have outlawed the inhaling of certain compounds with the intent of becoming intoxicated.

Because inhalants are not included in the Controlled Substances Act, they are not part of the U.S. Drug Enforcement Administration's Schedule of Drugs. This means that inhalants are not subject to the same government regulations and legal penalties for manufacture, possession, sale, and use that drugs such as cocaine and methamphetamines are.

Education

Education is the best way to prevent the abuse of inhalants. Studies have shown that many children and ado-

Adults need a better understanding of the fact than dangerous drugs aren't found only at parties and on city streets—they can also be on household shelves, in products that seem innocent.

lescents are simply not aware that sniffing, bagging, and huffing are dangerous practices. After all, the government approved the products they are inhaling. Of course the regulatory agencies did not intend them to be used to become intoxicated, but some individuals might believe that since they're safe for one use, they're okay to use in any way, shape, or form. Sadly, that can be a deadly misconception.

But, children and adolescents are not the only persons who should become educated about the dangers of inhalants and solvents. Parents often lack information as well. They need to

> National Inhalants and Poisons Awareness Week is held the third week of March.

be taught that sniffing is a serious problem (and not just with teens), and they may have everything their child needs to do it right in their homes.

Inhalants and Solvents—Sniffing Disaster 107

Children and adolescents need to learn about the dangers of inhalants. Parents need to be aware of the severity of the problem as well.

Schools are developing programs to educate students and parents about the problem and dangers of inhalant abuse. The National Inhalant Prevention Coalition (www.inhalants.org) has compiled a list of age-appropriate tips for teachers in how to help prevent inhalant abuse.

Ages 4 to 7:
- Teach about oxygen's importance to life and body functioning.
- Discuss the need for parental supervision and adequate room ventilation for cleaning products, solvents, glues and other products.
- Be a good role model; let students see you reading labels and following instructions.

Ages 7 to 10:
- Define and discuss the term "toxic"; students can practice reading labels and following instructions.
- Teach about oxygen's importance to life and functioning, with emphasis on body systems and brain functions.
- Discuss the need for parental supervision, following directions and adequate room ventilation.
- Be a good role model; let students see you reading labels and following instructions.
- Discuss and discourage "body pollution" and introducing poisons into the body.

Ages 10 to 14:
- Discuss negative effects of oxygen deprivation.
- Teach/reinforce peer resistance skills.
- Discuss environmental toxins and personal safety issues.

Ages 14 to 18:
- Describe and discuss implications of other gases replacing oxygen in the blood.
- Describe and discuss short/long-term effects of inhaling toxic products.
- Describe and discuss negative effects of volatile chemicals on fatty brain tissue.
- Where appropriate, offer access to counselor or other qualified professional.
- Respond to questions concerning specific products by describing negative effects and consequences.

In addition to the information listed above, there are some definite DOs and DON'Ts to school-based prevention programs.

DO
- ✓ Review school policy regarding drug use and referral service
- ✓ Provide training for all school staff as well as parents
- ✓ Start prevention efforts, by age 5, minimum
- ✓ Link inhalants to safety or environmental issues
- ✓ Ascertain current level of knowledge
- ✓ Teach and reinforce appropriate skills
    - reading labels
    - safety precautions
    - following directions
    - decision-making skills
    - recognition of poisons/toxins
    - refusal skills
    - awareness of physical symptoms

School-based programs are an important aspect of preventing inhalant abuse. The National Inhalant Prevention Coalition has recommended guidelines specific to different ages and grade levels.

Inhalants and Solvents—Sniffing Disaster

The Internet offers a lot of information on inhalants. However, not every website contains valid or current facts.

DON'T
- Ø Glamorize or promote usage
- Ø Rely on scare tactics
- Ø Tell too much, too soon
- Ø Give details on "how to use" or trendy products being abused
- Ø Limit prevention to secondary grade levels
- Ø Link inhalants with drugs or a drug unit

The Internet makes a vast amount of information available to anyone with computer access. Unfortunately, not all websites have the most up-to-date or accurate information. One must be a wary consumer of information, noting where the information comes from and if there is any *hidden agenda* by the authors or posters. This takes work, and perhaps some digging, but it's an important act of due diligence. Information found on government sites, or sites such as the National Inhalant Prevention Coalition (www.inhalants.org) can usually be trusted.

It's probably unlikely that we will ever live in an inhalant/solvent-free world. So, it is necessary to learn how to live with them, and the fact that there will likely always be people who choose to use them in order to get high. But, perhaps with intense education about their dangers, both immediate and long term, those numbers can get lower, and lower, and lower . . .

Inhalants and solvents are a part of our world. Therefore it is important that everyone is made aware of the dangers involved in abusing them.

Heads Up: Inhalants—A Quiz
(from *Scholastic Choices*, November 1, 2005)

Test your knowledge of inhalants. Choose the correct answer to each question.

1. Most inhalants are actually intended to be
   a. prescription drugs.
   b. household and office products.
   c. painkillers.
   d. cold medicine.
2. How do inhalants wind up in abusers' bloodstreams?
   a. Abusers inject them.
   b. Abusers breathe them in.
   c. Abusers take them in pill form.
   d. All of the above.
3. Some inhalants are safer than others.
   a. true
   b. false
4. Which of the following organs or body systems can be seriously damaged by inhalant abuse?
   a. the nervous system (brain, spinal cord, and nerves)
   b. the heart
   c. the liver
   d. all of the above
5. The inhalant nitrous oxide can rob the body of _____, causing death.
   a. blood
   b. essential vitamins
   c. dopamine
   d. oxygen
6. Which of the following is not a risk of inhalant abuse?
   a. hearing loss
   b. blackouts
   c. sudden sniffing death
   d. none of the above
7. Toluene, a chemical found in many inhalants, can cause muscle spasms, tremors, and hearing loss. It does so by breaking down
   a. a nerve coating called myelin.
   b. a section of the inner ear called the cochlea.
   c. the brain's balance center.
   d. nerve cells in the nose.

8. Benzene, a toxic component of gasoline fumes, can cause aplastic anemia, an often fatal disease of the
   a. liver.
   b. lungs.
   c. blood.
   d. brain.
9. When toxins from inhalants stay in the body for a long time, they are stored in
   a. fatty tissue.
   b. muscle tissue.
   c. the inner ear.
   d. the stomach.
10. A recent survey found that more than ___ of 8th-graders didn't realize that regular use of inhalants is harmful.
    a. 2 percent
    b. 8 percent
    c. 38 percent
    d. 66 percent

Answer key:
1. b; 2. b; 3. b; 4. d; 5. d; 6. d; 7. a; 8. c; 9. a; 10. c.

Glossary

Aboriginal: Pertaining to the original inhabitants of a country or region.

abstinence: The act of choosing not to give in to a craving for something.

anecdotal: Based only on reports or observations; usually from unscientific observers.

angina pectoris: A disease marked by brief attacks of severe chest pain, caused by deficient oxygen supply to the heart muscles.

antiquity: Referring to ancient times.

aplastic anemia: A condition when bone marrow stops producing new blood cells.

butane: A gaseous compound composed of carbon and hydrogen atoms; often used in cigarette lighters.

compromised: Impaired, damaged.

conducive: Tending to promote or assist.

contemptuous: Showing disdain; looking down on someone or something.

cyanide: A poison.

delusions: False psychotic beliefs about oneself or about other people and objects that are maintained despite evidence to the contrary.

dementia: Impaired functioning of the brain and thought processes; often to the point of madness or insanity.

diaphoresis: Excessive perspiration.

discernable: Able to be recognized or known.

efficacy: The power to produce a desired effect.

electroencephalogram (EEG): A test that records and traces brain waves.

electrolyte: A chemical, such as sodium or calcium, that regulates processes like the flow of nutrients into and waste products out of cells.

emanated: Came out from a source.

epidemiological: Relating to epidemiology, the science that studies the incidence, distribution, and control of diseases in a population.

euphoria: A feeling of extreme happiness.

fissure: A narrow opening or crack of considerable length and depth.

Great Depression: A worldwide economic downturn that started in 1929 and lasted through most of the 1930s.

greenhouse effect: A warming of the surface and lower atmosphere of the Earth caused by the accumulation of certain gases in the atmosphere.

hallucinations: Perceptions of objects and situations that are not real.

halocarbon: A compound made up of carbon and one or more of the halogen elements, which are fluorine, chlorine, bromine, iodine and astatine.

halogenated: Combined with or including one of the halogen elements.

hidden agenda: The true purpose behind an action; an ulterior motive.

indigenous: Native to an area, occurring naturally.

inert gas: Any of a group of gases, including helium and neon, that are very stable and have very low reaction rates.

inherent: Belonging by nature; part of the essential character of something.

inhibitions: The mental processes that impose restraint on behavior.

intravenous: Entering by way of a vein, as in injecting drugs into the bloodstream using a needle.

mitigate: To make less severe or harsh.

neurocognitive: Relating to the central nervous system and thinking abilities.

neuropathies: Diseases or abnormalities of the nervous system.

nystagmus: A rapid, involuntary back and forth movement of the eyeballs.

octane: An eight-carbon compound found in petroleum and used as a fuel and solvent.

oxidizer: An agent that removes an electron, creating a more positive charge, as when oxygen removes a hydrogen atom.

pallor: Paleness or absence of color, especially in the face.

pharmacological: Relating to the science that studies drugs and their origin, properties and reactions, especially with regards to their use as medicine.

photosensitivity: A sensitivity to light, especially sunlight.

plethora: Abundance or excess.

psychoactive: Affecting the mind or behavior.

psychosis: Derangement of the mind characterized by a loss of contact with reality, as in schizophrenia.

sedatives: Drugs having a calming or tranquilizing effect.

tachycardia: A heart rate faster than normal resting rate, whether after exercise or because of disease.

vaporize: To convert into the gaseous state as opposed the liquid or solid state; boil water to vaporize it into steam.

vasodilator: An chemical that widens blood vessels.

veritable: Being truly or very much so.

whippets: Cartridges designed to deliver nitrous oxide in a whipped cream dispenser.

Further Reading

Aretha, David. *Inhalants*. Berkeley Heights, N.J.: MyReportLinks.com, 2005.

Bankston, John. *Inhalants = Busted!* New York: Enslow, 2006.

Connolly, Sean. *Inhalants*. New York: Franklin Watts, 2005.

Fitzhugh, Karla. *Inhalants*. Chicago, Ill.: Raintree, 2003.

Lawton, Sandra Augustyn (ed.). *Drug Information for Teens*. Detroit, Mich.: Omnigraphics, 2006.

Lobo, Ingrid A. *Inhalants*. New York: Chelsea House, 2004.

Markovitz, Hal. *Inhalants*. Farmington Hills, Mich.: Lucent, 2005.

Menhard, Francha Roffe. *The Facts About Inhalants*. Tarrytown, N.Y.: Marshall Cavendish, 2004.

O'Donnell, Kerri. *Inhalants and Your Nasal Passages: The Incredibly Disgusting Story*. New York: Rosen, 2001.

For More Information

Above the Influence
www.abovetheinfluence.com/facts/drugs-inhalants.aspx

Focus Adolescent Services
www.focusas.com

National Inhalant Prevention Coalition
www.inhalants.org

National Institute on Drug Abuse: Inhalants
www.drugabuse.gov/infofacts/inhalants.html

Teen Drug Abuse
www.teen-drug-abuse.org/inhalant-abuse.htm

The websites listed on this page were active at the time of publication. The publisher is not responsible for websites that have changed their addresses or discontinued operation since the date of publication. The publisher will review and update the website list upon each reprint.

Bibliography

Anderson, Carrie E., and Glenn A. Loomis. "Recognition and Prevention of Inhalant Abuse." *American Family Physician* 68, no. 5(September 2003).

Clancy, Natalie. "Sheshatshiu: An Innu Community's Battle with Addiction." CBC News Online, December 14, 2004. http://www.cbc.ca.news.background/aboriginals/sheshatshiu.html.

Division of Alcohol and Drug Abuse. "As a Matter of Fact . . . Inhalants." http://www.well.com/user/woa/fsinhale.htm.

"Drug Information: What Are Inhalants?" http://www.narconon.ca/inhalants.htm.

Hanson, Glen R. "Rising to the Challenge of Inhalant Abuse." http://www.drugabuse.gov/NIDA_notes/NNVol17N4/DirRepVol17.html.

"Heads Up: Inhalants—A Quiz." *Scholastic Choices*. November 1, 2005.

"Inhalants." http://faculty.washington.edu/chudler/inhale.html.

"Inhalants." http://www.coolnurse.com/inhalants.htm.

"Inhalants." http://www.streetdrugs.org/inhalants.htm.

"Inhalants: Stats, Signs, & More Info." *Science World*, March 7, 2003.

Kaufman, Timothy. "Inhalants." http://www.emedicine.com/NEURO/topic173.htm.

Mathias, Robert. "Chronic Solvent Abusers Have More Brain Abnormalities and Cognitive Impairments Than Cocaine Abusers." http://www.drugabuse.gov/NIDA_notes/NNVol17N4/Chronic.html.

Missouri Department of Mental Health. "Fact Sheet: Inhalants." http://www.well.com/user/woa/fsinhale.htm.

National Inhalant Prevention Coalition. "Solvents in the School." http://www.inhalants.org/school.htm.

National Inhalant Prevention Coalition. "State Inhalant Legislation." http://www.inhalants.org/laws.htm.

National Inhalant Prevention Coalition. "Tips for Teachers." http://www.inhalants.org/teacher.htm.

The National Institute on Drug Abuse. "Facts About Inhalant Abuse." http://www.drugabuse.gov/NIDA_Notes/NNVol15N6/tearoff.html.

The National Institute on Drug Abuse. "Inhalant Abuse Among Young People." http://www.drugabuse.gov/NIDA_notes/NNVol17N4/tearoff.html.

The National Institute on Drug Abuse. "Inhalant Abuse Is an Emerging Public Health Problem." http://www.nida.nih.gov/about/welcome/messageInhalants105.html.

The National Institute on Drug Abuse. "Inhalants." http://www/nida.nih.gov/DrugPages/Inhalants.html.

The National Institute on Drug Abuse. "NIDA InfoFacts: Inhalants." http://www.nida.nih.gov/Infofacts/Inhalants.html.

The National Institute on Drug Abuse. "NIDA Research Identifies Factors Related to Inhalant Abuse, Addiction." http://www.drugabuse.gov/Newsroom/04/NR9-28.html.

The National Institute on Drug Abuse. "Teen Drug Use Declines 2003–2004—But Concerns Remain About Inhalants and Painkillers." http://www.drugabuse.gov/Newsroom/04/NR12-21.html.

The National Youth Anti-Drug Campaign. "Inhalants." http://www.theantidrug.com/drug_info/drug_info_inhalants.asp.

Office of National Drug Control Policy. "Drug Facts: Inhalants." http://www.whitehousedrugpolicy.gov/drugfact/inhalants/index.html.

Partnership for a Drug-Free America. "Addicted to Inhalants." Teens: Stories, Info & Help. http://www.drugfree.org/Teen/teen_3.html."

"Poison Vapors: The Truth About Inhalants: Inhalants Can Cause Harm to the Whole Body, Including Long-Lasting Damage to the Brain, Physical Disabilities, and Even Death." *Scholastic Choices*, November 11, 2005.

Spelete, Heidi. "Do Not Overlook Inhalant Use in Adolescents: Most Teens Are Unaware that 'Huffing' from a Can of Spray Paint of Keyboard Cleaner Can Be Catastrophic." *Family Practice News*, April 15, 2006.

Stark, Kenneth D. "Minority Adolescents and Substance Use Risk/Protective Factors: A Focus on Inhalant Use." *Adolescence*, September 22, 2004.

Substance Abuse and Mental Health Services Administration, Office of Applied Studies. Drug Abuse Warning Network, 2004: National Estimates of Drug-Related Emergency Department Visits (DAWN series D-28, DHHS Publication No. SMA 06-4143). Rockville, Md.: Author, 2006.

Substance Abuse and Mental Health Services Administration, Office of Applied Studies. National Survey on Drug Use and Health: The NSDUH Report. Rockville, Md.: Author, 2006.

"Top 10 Things You Need to Know About Inhalants." *Junior Scholastic*, January 5, 2004.

U.S. Department of Health and Human Services, Substance Abuse and Mental Health Services Administration. "Tips for Teens: The Truth About Inhalants." http://ncadi.samhsa.gov/govpubs/phd631.html.

U.S. Drug Enforcement Administration. "Inhalants." http://www.dea.gov/concern/inhalants.html.

Worcester, Sharon. "Survey: Teens Use Inhalants More, Worry About Risks Less." *Clinical Psychiatry News* (2006).

Young, Leah. "Inhalant Use Can Lead to Illegal Drugs, Study Says." *Drug Detection Report*, March 31, 2005.

Index

aerosol propellants 12, 13

behavioral treatment 89, 90

Canada 57, 71–75, 102, 130
Centers for Disease Control and Prevention (CDC) 54
central nervous system (CNS) 31, 32, 41
Controlled Substances Act (CSA) 106

detoxification 80, 83, 93

First Nations 71–75, 102, 103
fluorocarbon 26

gases 13

Monitoring the Future (MTF) 52, 53

Narcotics Anonymous 90–93
National Inhalant Prevention Coalition 29, 44, 59, 65, 66, 93, 109, 113
National Institute on Drug Abuse (NIDA) 34, 35, 84

National Native Youth Solvent Addiction (NNYSA) 102, 103
National Survey on Drug Use and Health (NSDUH) 53, 54, 68
Native Americans 68, 71
nerve cells 32, 33
nitrites 13, 15
nitrous oxide 26, 29

Oracle of Delphi 17–21

pharmacological treatment 90, 99, 102
Pythia 18–21

side effects 37–43, 45
street names 44, 45

toluene 24
treatment 77–103
Twelve Steps 91–93

volatile solvents 11–13

Picture Credits

DEA 51, 107
fotolia.com 33, 34, 37, 64, 84, 92, 109
    Sascha Burkhard 67
    Przemyslaw Ceglarek 58
    Jacek Chabraszewski 101
    Roman Dekan 38
    Chris Harvey 110
    Mat Hayward 112
    Jenny Holmlund 89
    Milan Jurkovic 80
    Oktay Ortakcioglu 46
    Edyta Pawlawska 106
    Stas Perov 90
    Vova Pomortzeff 48
    Hazel Proudlove 97
    Radu Razvan 42
    Robert Redelowski 69
    Mike Thompson 40
    John Tomaselli 74
    Graca Victoria 27
    Vasiliy Yakobchuk 31
    Lisa F. Young 95
istock.com 22
    Henry Chaplin 83
    Brandon Miokovic 22
Jupiter Images 8, 10, 14, 18, 20, 28, 30, 55, 60, 63, 68, 70, 79

To the best knowledge of the publisher, all other images are in the public domain. If any image has been inadvertently uncredited, please notify Harding House Publishing Services, Vestal, New York 13850, so that rectification can be made for future printings.

Author and Consultant Biographies

Author

Noa Flynn was born and raised in the Midwest. She moved east to attend Syracuse University and never left. She currently lives in Upstate New York, where she is a freelance writer, specializing in nonfiction books and articles.

Series Consultant

Jack E. Henningfield, Ph.D., is a professor at the Johns Hopkins University School of Medicine, and he is also Vice President for Research and Health Policy at Pinney Associates, a consulting firm in Bethesda, Maryland, that specializes in science policy and regulatory issues concerning public health, medications development, and behavior-focused disease management. Dr. Henningfield has contributed information relating to addiction to numerous reports of the U.S. Surgeon General, the National Academy of Sciences, and the World Health Organization.